T0064032

HEBREW WORD STUDY

A Hebrew Teacher Finds
Rest in the Heart of God

Chaim Bentorah

Order this book online at www.trafford.com
or email orders@trafford.com

Most Trafford titles are also available at major online book retailers.

Printed in the United States of America.

ISBN: 978-1-4907-1546-9 (sc)
ISBN: 978-1-4907-1547-6 (e)

Trafford rev. 09/25/2013

Trafford
PUBLISHING® www.trafford.com

North America & international
toll-free: 1 888 232 4444 (USA & Canada)
fax: 812 355 4082

TABLE OF CONTENTS

Preface

WITH THE ADVENT OF multiple modern English translations
of the Bible being published over the last fifty years,
Christians have come to realize that there can be a wide range
of meanings and renderings of various words from the Bible
in the original language. As a Hebrew teacher and student
of ancient languages one of the most common questions I get
is, "What is the best translation?" This is usually followed by
the question, "Which translation is the closest to the original
Biblical language?" The answer I give to both questions is,
"All of them."

With few exceptions, every translation and paraphrase
of the Bible is done with much scholarship and prayer by
the translators. Every translator is convinced that he or she
has presented the best renderings for each word and firmly
believes they have given the rendering that is closest to the
original language.

So we now ask the question as to why there are some
many differences in each translation of the Bible. The answer
to that can be anything from a translator reading his own
theological persuasion, bias or prejudice into his translations
to the purpose and/or intention behind the translation. By
this I mean is the translator going for a literal word of word

translation, attempting to put his translation into modern thought, trying to put his translation into a cultural context, trying to present a paraphrase, a commentary or any number of different purposes and/or intentions for working on a new translation. Ultimately, the answer as to why there are so many different translations lies in something that happened almost two thousand and five hundred years ago. From 597 BC to 538 BC the Jewish nation was taken into captivity. During this captivity time the language of Jewish people, which was Hebrew, assimilated into the Babylonian culture and Hebrew became a dead language, preserved only for ceremonial purposes. A dead language means that it is no longer a language used for every day conversation. When this happens the meanings behind many words become lost and its original intent may never be positively identified. It is left to scholars and linguist to offer their best educated guess. Rarely is there one hundred percent agreement on every rendering, although a majority opinion can exist for many words and we can be relatively certain of their renderings. But for every such word there are words whose renderings are hotly debated among scholars.

After Hebrew died, Aramaic became the common language of the people and was the common language spoken in Israel at the time of Christ. Jesus came from Galilee which was located in the Northern territory of Israel where they spoke a Northern or Old Galilean dialect of Hebrew which was more idiomatic and colloquial than the Southern dialect spoken in Judea where the Pharisees and other religious leaders lived. Up until just a few years ago it was believed that the Old Galilean Aramaic dialect was also a dead language until it was discovered that a tribe of people in Northern Iraq still spoke this dialect. There is an intense study being done today into this language which is opening up a deeper and greater understanding of the Gospels. There is much debate over whether the Gospels were originally written in Aramaic or Greek, but there seems to be a general agreement that Jesus spoke Aramaic and thus, even if the Gospels were not written in Aramaic, the writers would have had to translate the Aramaic words of Jesus into Greek to write them down.

If we cannot even agree as to what language the Gospels were written in, how can we even begin to understand the true meaning and intent of the words that were spoken during a different time and a different culture? For this reason I believe it is very important that our seminaries and Bible Colleges take a serious look at requiring our future Christian leaders to not only study Greek and Hebrew but Aramaic as well.

That is a New Testament issue however, but what of the Old Testament? This was written in Hebrew except for portions of the Book of Daniel and the Book of Ezra which were written in Aramaic. Hebrew, by the mere fact that it is a dead language, leaves us open to much debate as to proper modern English word to apply to an ancient word that has been dead for twenty five hundred years.

When it comes to dealing with a dead language we are at the mercy of our linguist and various other scholars to guide us into tracing the origins and roots of an ancient dead language. A translator must not ignore the science of linguistics when translating the Word of God. Yet, any schooled linguist will tell you that the translations you finally arrive at are still just man's best guess. The proof of this lies in the numerous modern English translations of the Bible that we have today. They are all good, even excellent and well documented translations, translated by skilled translators and yet they all have subtle differences because their final translations are still man's best guess.

In my first book, *A Hebrew Teacher's Search for the Heart of God*, I tended to do my word studies based upon the traditional approaches to translations. This would be to study the best guesses of man found in translations, lexicons and dictionaries. In my second book, *A Hebrew Teacher Explores the Heart of God*; I started to move away from the Western mindset and started to approach the Word of God with a more Eastern or Semitic mindset. This meant less dependence on the opinions of man and more on the heart of God and what I felt the Holy Spirit was teaching me personally. The West is a very technological and scientific culture. We examine everything in light of the scientific method. This involves building on the research and study of former scientists. The mind rules over the heart in scientific research, as it must. Science is built on facts and what can be proven with the eye. The decisions of the heart are only used when no evidence or facts exist and a conclusion must be reached. Even with our art, most people in the Western world judge a song by how technically accurate it is played or sung. They listen with their minds to judge whether all the right notes were struck, or if the timing was right, and a breath taken in the right place. Art is examined by how technically accurate each brush stroke is made or how the final product fits our concept of perfection. To the general public of the

Western world, and to the frustration of the artist, art is judged by the mind and not the heart. In Western culture the mnd comes before the heart. Yet, I have found that often in Eastern or Semitic thought, the heart comes before the mind. Thus, in my second book I tried to create a balance in my word studies between my heart and God's heart and my mind.

Now, in my third book, after having discovered and explored God's heart, I have found myself letting God's heart rule my mind in my word studies. I believe, in this book I have left the Western mindset and began to really enter into an Eastern or Semitic mindset in my word studies. I began to feel a freedom to allow God's heart to rule my mind. When I did this I discovered that I was no longer *searching* or *exploring* the Heart of God, I was now *resting* in the Heart of God.

Hebrew Alphabet

א	ALEPH
ב	BETH
ג	GIMMEL
ד	DALETH
ה	HEI
ו	VAV
ז	ZAYIN
ח	CHETH
ט	TETH
י	YOD
כ	KAP
ל	LAMED
מם	MEM
נ	NUN

ס	**SAMEK**
ע	**AYIN**
פ	**PEI**
צ	**SADE**
ק	**QUF**
ר	**RESH**
ש	**SHIN, SINE**
ת	**TAW**
?	**MYSTERY LETTER**

Day 1

Rest (Shabbat)

EXODUS 16:30: "So THE people rested on the seventh day."

Rest—Hebrew: *shabat*—rest, to cease, be still, to interrupt,

The word *rest* in this passage is *vayishevethu*. From the root word *shabat* which means to rest and to cease. We learn in Genesis 2:2 that God "rested" on the seventh day. I mean all that creating into being must have worn poor God out, surely God needed a rest; I know I would have. The English rendering for the word *shabat* as "rest" can be a little misleading. It is not to rest to regain your strength, it is to "cease" from your activity or to interrupt your normal activity to accomplish something. What are you to accomplish on the Sabbath? Used here in Exodus you have a sort of play the word *yashev* that means to dwell, or sit down. Shabot has a numerical value of 702. The word *macoreth* also has a numerical value of 702 and means *to bond*. This time of *resting* is meant to bond with God. You don't bond with God by worrying or fretting over the pressures and problems of the past week. You bond with God by wandering through the Alphabet.

1

The word *shabat* is spelled "Shin, Beth, and Taw." In Hebrew, every word is built upon a three-letter root word. Some words are interrelated when they share the same first two letters. In this case, the first two letters of *Shabat* are Shin, Beth. All the other words that start with Shin and Beth will in some way related to the Shin Beth Taw or rest. Twelve other words in Hebrew begin with Shin Beth. In other words, we are to take one day a week and rest or cease from our normal activity to do twelve things. When you celebrate the Sabbath next Sunday or Saturday or whichever day you celebrate the Sabbath, remember the twelve other Shin Beth words which tell you what you are to do or what God wishes to accomplish on this seventh day that you cease from your normal activity.

Shin Beth—Aleph—*Shava'*: God's passion. The first letter of the alphabet is Aleph and represents God. Shin Beth Aleph refers to God's passionate love. The first thing you are to do on this day of rest is to just sit back and let God love you, and enjoy His passionate love.

Shin Beth—Beth—*Shavav*: Kindle a fire. The next thing you are to do on the Sabbath is Shavav, which is to allow God's passionate love to kindle a fire of love and affection for Him in return.

Shin Beth—Hei—*Shavah*: To take as captive, to be taken away as a bride. When you and God love each other he will take you as his personal captive, take you away as a bride to His bridal chamber to be intimate with you.

Shin Beth—Chet—*Shavach*: To sooth, calm, relax, and calm you nerves. When He takes you away as His bride and loves on you, you will become Shavach, the pressures and

2

stresses of the prior six days will settle down, be soothed and you will find your frayed nerves calming down.

Shin Beth—Teth—*Shavat*: To measure. Once in the bridal chamber God measures you. He will examine you as a husband would examine and measure the beauty of his bride.

Shin Beth—Kap—*Shavak*: To mingle, interweave, have intercourse. After a time of just enjoying the beauty of His bride, God will then share an intimacy with you as His bride.

Shin Beth—Lamed—*Shaval*: To grow. During this time of intimacy God and you as His bride will grow closer together, more in love, more passionate with each other.

Shin Beth—Nun—*Shavan*: To be tender, to be delicate. During this time of intimacy, it will be time when God speaks tenderly to you as His bride. He will speak of love. He will call you His dearest, sweetheart and other delicate names.

Shin Beth—Mem—*Shavam*: To share hidden secrets, hidden knowledge. When two lovers are being intimate together, speaking lovingly to each other, they cannot help but share their deepest secrets, sharing things that they would share with no one else. Thus during this Sabbath rest God will share the secrets of His heart with you as His bride.

Shin Beth—Ayin—*Shava'*: To become satisfied, fulfilled. After a time of sharing love, intimacy, and the secrets of each other's hearts you as bride will feel this great, overwhelming sense of satisfaction and fulfillment.

Shin Beth—Sade—*Shavats*: To weave or intermingle together to create something beautiful. During this time of intimacy, God and you as His bride will intermingle together, weave together to create something beautiful in your relationship.

Shin Beth—Resh—*Shavar*: To examine in order to make pure. As the Sabbath concludes, God will do a final examination of His bride and declare that you are indeed pure and holy before Him.

So, as you conclude your celebration of the next Sabbath, perhaps you can wander through Hebrew alphabet and let God tell you what you mean to Him and you tell Him what He means to you.

Day 2

Drew Me Out (Yamesheni)

Psalms 18:16: "He sent from above, he took me, he drew me out of many waters."

Some translations, or paraphrases actually, will render the word *shalach (sent)* as reached down. I like that poetic expression as it pictures us struggling in a raging sea and God reaching down from heaven and picking us up out of the raging seas. There is no doubt that this is implied in this passage, but it is not what the verse is really saying. It is saying so much more and expressing something even more wonderful than just reaching down to rescue us.

The Aramaic form of the word *shalach* means to *reach out* and the particular form that is used here, if it were in Aramaic, would be a Peal form, which would intensify the verb making it very definite. If you were struggling in a raging sea God would, without question, pull you out.

Yet this is in Hebrew and *shalach* is in a simple Qal imperfect form. The word *shalach* means to *send away, or to detach oneself, or something from you*. It is a word used for *divorce*. It has a basic idea of separating oneself from something with a specific purpose or mission. It is in an imperfect form, which means *He will separate Himself from above*. There is almost a hidden Messianic message in this verse. We are struggling in a raging sea and God will one day separate Himself from heaven and come to earth to rescue us. He will leave that heavenly helicopter and jump right into the raging sea with us to rescue us.

The verse further explains that He will not only *draw us* out of the waters, but He will *take us* and then He will *draw us* out of the many waters. The word for *take* in Hebrew is the word *laqak*. Sure the word means to *take*, but it means much more than that; it means to take as a possession, to take something that is of extreme value to you or to others. It is the same word used when a Jewish man announces joyfully, "I have *taken (laqak)* myself a bride". In fact, the word *laqak* itself means to *take a wife*. The picture is not one of God just reaching down from heaven and grabbing hold of us and pulling us out of the raging sea, it is a picture of God leaping from that helicopter, jumping into the sea, putting his arms around us, protecting us while we are still in that sea and then grabbing hold of that cable and bringing us back into the helicopter or to heaven with Him. Yet, He is pictured as more than just some brave coast guardsman rescuing us from a raging sea; He is a lover, rescuing His beloved from the dangerous waters.

Oh, but the next words are even more telling, it is the word for *drew me out*. The word *drew me out* in Hebrew is *yamesheni* which has two possible roots with an amazing play on words. It could be *mashah*, which is the same root for the name *Moses* and means to draw out or deliver. If this were the root, it would be in a Hiphil form and would suggest that

God would do something that would cause us to be taken out or delivered from the raging sea. Again, there is a very Messianic suggestion picturing his death on the cross and resurrection as this would be an act to cause us to be rescued. You could almost picture something more from the word *Mashah*. At first glance, it looks like the word *Mashach* where we get the word Messiah except the last letter, the Chet, is *broken*; that is, there is a space in the upper left hand corner of the Chet making it a Hei. The *Hei* is referred to by the ancient sages as the *broken letter*. Perhaps God is sending us a message that He will send his only begotten son to die on a cross to rescue us from the raging sea and that His motive is out of brokenness, He is suffering such a broken heart over our sinful situation pictured as drowning in a raging sea that He is going to separate Himself from His secure and safe heaven and come down personally to rescue us and in fact to give His very life to save us.

There is another possible root word for *yamesheni*, which offers an intriguing play on words for that root word would be *mashash*, which means to tenderly touch or feel. It is used for one who is carefully examining a wound. When Jesus jumps into that raging sea to rescue us, He will first carefully and tenderly touch us, feel us and examine us for any wounds that He will need to heal. Yes, He will examine our own wounds and heal them while ignoring all the wounds that He suffered on the cross.

DAY 3

Hide ('Alam)

Isaiah 1: 15-16: "And when ye spread forth your hands, I will hide mine eyes from you: yea, when ye make many prayers, I will not hear: your hands are full of blood. Wash you, make yourself clean; put away the evil of your doings from before my eyes; cease to do evil;"

This morning I read an article in the news about a man who spent the last four years of his life writing out the entire Bible by hand. He would sometimes spend up to fourteen hours a day on this project, writing every day, seven days a week. After spending the last six years in my search for the heart of God writing out Hebrew words as they related to specific passages of Scripture, spending a minimum of four hours day on my project, I can only assume that for this man's project to take four years, he must have carefully written out every word making it as neat as possible and mediating on each word as he wrote them out. He says he started this project as a way of studying the Word of God and that as a result he found himself becoming more patient, peaceful and loving. One would tend to think that this project was some sort of ritual, like reciting prayer repeatedly, offering sacrifices over and over. It would be the very thing that Isaiah was condemning in Isaiah 1. I suppose the same could be said for my obsession with the Word of God, except for one thing. Isaiah is not condemning the ritualistic practices; he is condemning the motives behind them. I mean why would God command His people to perform sacrifices and then call them an abomination? (Verse 13) Isaiah is basically accusing the people of Israel of performing these rituals and prayers to manipulate God, not to worship Him.

Note that that Isaiah is saying that when you "spread forth your hands". The word *spread* in Hebrew comes from the root word *parash* which has the preposition *Beth* and the word for *hands* is *pei* (palms) not *yad* (hands). Hence, this would be rendered as "in the spreading of your palms". This is the gesture of the ancient Hebrews when they make a request unto God, they would hold out their hands with their palms facing up as if to receive something. It is sort of like a beggar who extends his hands to you.

You do not have to live for long in Chicago to know that many, if not most of the beggars who approach you with outstretched hands know where the closest mission, Salvation Army, church or public agency is located. In many cases, it is fairly obvious that these beggars are not looking for their next meal but to feed their addiction. When such a person approaches me, I do exactly as God says he does when we come begging to Him for something that has other than pure motives; I turn my head and act like I do not see that person. Hence, that is what God means when he says he will *hide his eyes*. The word *hide* is *'alam* which means to conceal

9

or make a secret. He is not being cruel; he is just practicing tough love and refusing to feed your sinful addiction.

I remember talking once with one of these street people and he told me that he looks for people who will make eye contact with him. He knows if he can make eye contact with someone, that person has some sense of compassion and will immediately become (for want of a better word) a *mark*. This is someone who can easily be manipulated and will find it hard to refuse his request. This is why God will hide or conceal His eyes. God is completely filled with compassion for our problems, but He will *conceal His eyes* so that He will not be manipulated. The word *'alam (hide)* in this verse is preceded by an Aleph which puts this word in a Hiphal imperfect form. Hence, God is saying that He will be caused to conceal His eyes. In other words, our impure motives, our attempts to manipulate God with our prayers, sacrifices, offerings, tithes, and even worship causes *(Hiphal)* God to conceal His eyes.

God goes further, "When you make many prayers, I will not hear." The word for *many* in Hebrew is *rachah* and also found in a Hiphal imperfect form. The word *rachah* means to increase in numbers and/or in intensity. The word *hear is shama*, which means to respond or obey. Hence, this could be rendered as "when you increase the numbers and intensity of your prayers, I will still not respond". I have heard preachers and Christians *shout* their prayers, filling them with intensity, trying to make them sound powerful. Yet, if done to manipulate God or patronize Him, He will not respond.

Literally, what God is saying in this verse is, "Don't try to manipulate me, don't patronize me. Don't think you will get anywhere by telling me that I am wonderful, great, and powerful, I know that already. Don't try to manipulate me by pretending to be pious with outstretched palms trying to be humble; I know your heart and motives. Don't try to bribe me with your tithes, offerings, and sacrifices, I own the cattle on a thousand hills, I don't need your pennies.

You want me to hear you then wash and clean up your motives. Put away all your *evil*."

This word for *evil* in Hebrew is *ra'a'*, which is an evil of impure, selfish motives. The word *wash* is *rachats* in Hebrew, which means to cleanse. The word in Aramaic gives a little more insight as it has the idea of *trust*. *Rachats* has the idea cleansing yourself from trusting in the wrong things, like your manipulative abilities. The word for *clean* is *sakak*, which is preceded by a Hei and a Chirik putting this in a Hithpael form. The word *sakak* means cleansing or becoming innocent. In other words, if your prayers are to be heard then you must change your motives, stop trying to manipulate, or bribe God and *make yourself innocent (Hithapel)*. That is, to have pure motives. You do that by building a relationship with God and you build a relationship with God the same way you build a relationship with anyone else; you spend time with that person and listen to what they have to say.

This takes us back to our gentleman who spent four years writing out the Bible. The Word of God had a cleansing, peaceful and loving effect on him because it is the Word of God. The Talmud teaches that the Torah will purify your motives. The more time you spend in the Word and in prayer, the more your motives will be cleansed and the least likely you will be to try and manipulate or bribe God.

Building a relationship takes time, effort and sacrifice. To have a solid relationship with someone that person must be on the top of your priority list. So too with God, He is not another pill in your medicine closet that your run to when you have a headache, He is a friend, parent and lover who needs our love and attention in return.

Day 4

House—Place of the Heart (Bayith)

Psalms 127:1: A song of Ascent for Solomon: "Unless the Lord builds the house, they labor in vain that build it."

Solomon's Temple was called "Solomon's Temple" for good reason. This was more Solomon's temple than it was God's temple with regard to the construction. Up until recently, all we really knew about the first temple was what we were able to glean from Scripture. Since the return of the Jews to Israel and Israel gaining control of Jerusalem, there has been and continues to be extensive research going on in regards to Solomon's Temple.

For one thing, we know that the temple was built on the backs of slave labor. We find that Solomon taxed the people to the point of rebellion to finance the temple. We have discovered that there was no silver used in the temple although it was commanded by God that certain things be made of silver, Solomon chose to make them of gold. Some of the things that were supposed to be made of gold, Solomon commanded they be made of brass or copper. This ended up being more of a monument to Solomon than to God. By the time of the dedication of the temple Solomon had married a number of pagan wives who brought idolatry into Israel. It was barely more than five years after his death that his son, Rehoboam took much of the gold from the temple to bribe the Egyptians. In less than one lifetime after the dedication of the temple, it was in decline.

Prophets arose to warn of coming judgment. The people would mock and say, "Why look at the temple, we are the people of God, do you honestly think God would allow this beautiful monument to Himself be destroyed? Come on use some common sense". Common sense or not, it was destroyed.

Yet, when the temple was dedicated, we learn that God's presence filled it. Many traveled to the temple to sincerely worship God and God's glory filled the house despite the fact that it was not built according to His specifications and despite the fact that there was corruption among the priests.

"Unless the Lord build the house, they labor in vain that build it." The word we translate as *unless* is Hebrew word *im*, which is more commonly rendered as *if.* The syntax is a little confusing. You have two constructs together. "If Jehovah" and "he is not building". It appears the KJV is right on target with the syntax, except there is no definite article on the word *bayith (house)* and hence we should add a personal pronoun to our rendering: "If Jehovah is not building His house". The word house, *bayith,* in Jewish culture also expresses the idea of the place of the heart. You know the old saying: "Home is where the heart is". More clearly rendered you could say, "If Jehovah is not building a place within His heart . . ."

Then we add the last part, "They labor in vain who build it". This gave me pause in my quest for the heart of God. The temple was meant to be a place where you entered the heart of God. Yet, man corrupted the place, Solomon filled it with his own designs and yet God still let his presence be known, even though it was in a steady decline. The Apostle Paul tells us our bodies are the temple of God. The heart of God is meant to reside in us. Indeed, we do labor to build and maintain this temple. Often our labors are to bring glory to God in ministry. Yet, like Solomon, we cannot help but put a little of our own design into this temple. We cannot help but build a monument to ourselves. Sure, we seek to bring honor to God in our ministry, but deep inside we also want a little of that honor for ourselves, we want maybe to make a good living at it, or develop a reputation and a following. So what is so wrong with getting a little praise and honor for our labors? Maybe nothing is wrong with that except we do run the risk of a legacy that becomes "Solomon's Temple" and not "God's Temple". If that is the case all our labors whether in ministry or at secular jobs are in vain. The word *vain* in Hebrew is *shave*, which has the idea of *desolate or waste*. Our labor to build a place within God's heart is all a waste.

Jesus said in John 14:2: "In my father's house are many dwelling places. I go to prepare a place for you." Jesus spoke in the Old Galilean dialect of Aramaic. The Aramaic Bible, Peshitta, uses the word *bt* which we render as *house*, yet, like Hebrew *bt* could also be used to express the idea *of the place of the heart* which is identical to Hebrew word *bayith (house)* which is the word used in Psalms 127. Jesus may very well have said, "In my Father's heart are many rooms". Only He can build that place in His heart for us. If we try to build that place with all our ministries and monuments to ourselves, our labors are all wasted.

15

Day 5

Shortening of the Way (Kefitzat Haderech)

GENESIS 24:42: "BEHOLD I stand here by the well of water . . ."

Matthew 24:22: "And unless those days be shortened, no flesh shall be saved. But for the elect sake, those days will be shortened."

Kefitzat Haderech: A shortening of the way

Kefitzat Haderech is not found in the Bible, but there are ancient sages and rabbis who do believe it is mentioned in the Bible. Genesis 24:22 is one such verse. "Natsav 'avos" is translated in almost every English translation as if it were in a perfect tense or a completed action. "I came today". However, "Natsav'vo" is a participle and should be rendered "I am coming". More than that, as a participle it has the idea of both standing and coming at the same time. Such an expression is transcending time and only God can do both at the same time. Hence, translators just simply say he was standing. Yet, can man really "natsav 'vo" in a participle form? Many sages teach that this expression is a reference to *Kefitzat Haderech*. Literally translated it means a "shortening of the way".

Shmuel Yosef Aganon (an Israeli Nobel Prize winner for literature in 1966) wrote of a righteous rabbi who was given the gift of *Kefitzat Haderech* or the ability to transport himself from one place to another. He would transport himself into the treasury of the Habsburg Empire and help himself to some gold coins and then transport himself out before anyone could see him. He had to use the coins to help the poor. If he ever kept any for himself, if he ever used his gift for self-gain, even to receive praise and feed his pride, he would lose the gift of *Kefitzat Haderech*.

There are orthodox rabbis today who actually believe that God still gives the gift of *Kefitzat Haderech*. They point to the particular grammatical context of Genesis 24:42 and show that this servant completed his journey in one day, which was impossible unless he had the gift of *Kefitzat Haderech*.

In fact, Enoch, Elijah, Samuel, Ezekiel, Phillip and Jesus all demonstrated *Kefitzat Haderech*. In the Aramaic, it appears that what is being described in Matthew 24:22 is the concept of Kefitzat *Haderech*. Jesus says that for the elect sake the days will be shortened. Could Jesus have been speaking about *Kefitzat Haderech* as a gift available for saints living in the last days as a means of protection and evangelization?

What fascinates me more than anything about this is that the concept of *Kefitzat Haderech* transcends time. God does not live in time. God created time. Time for us will one day cease. We cannot, in our human state, grasp the idea of no end or no beginning, yet the very existence of the universe proves the idea of no beginning or end.

God is living in a constant state of *Kefitzat Haderech*. It is through *Kefitzat Haderech* that He is able to be omnipresent and to be able to spend every moment and second, 24/7, with you personally.

We are told we entertain angels unaware (Hebrew 13:2). Is it possible these are not supernatural beings but believers who move through time and space in an instant as "messengers" of God to be in a certain place at a certain time to help us along? Like this righteous rabbi in Shmuel Yoesf Aganon story, if they use the gift for self-gain or pride they will lose it and hence they would never reveal their gift of *Kefitat Haderech* and we would never learn they had such a gift.

Oh well, I didn't mean to waste your time with crazy Sci Fi stuff. I only wanted to give you a Biblical reference to point out that God indeed lives in a constant state of *Kefitzat Haderech* so that we are assured that He is with us every single moment of every day.

DAY 6

Murmur (Layan)

NUMBERS 14:27: "How LONG shall I bear with this evil congregation that murmurs against me? I have heard the murmurings of the children of Israel which they murmur against me."

Some modern translations say the children of Israel grumbled against God, others say they complained, and still others say that they made an outcry. Bad Israel, how dare they grumble, murmur, complain or even make an outcry against God after all the mighty miracles he did for them. You surely can't blame God for not being able to *bear* such an evil congregation. I know if I were God, my patience would surely run pretty thin against a nation that would keep demanding more and more and then belly ache because they did not get enough.

Is it the fact that Israel was acting like a spoiled child that made God declare they were *evil*? What did he mean by *evil* anyways? Was God's patience really running thin? Were the children of Israel really grumbling, complaining, murmuring and making an outcry to God?

I read this verse and I think of a Bible study I once attended where they were going through a workbook. Everyone seemed quite excited over the fact that they were actually studying one of those obscure books of the Bible that nobody ever reads, the Book of Numbers. One of the blanks in the workbook to fill in was, "God called the children of Israel evil because _____? Well that was an easy one, because they were murmuring against God. Some asked, "What does it mean to murmur." Immediately the response was: "Well, my translation says . . ." I thought, "Oh jolly, why here is a group who really wants to think and dig deep". I was really pleased until I heard someone ask: "Why is it that after all the miracles would someone complain against God?" That was when someone said: "Because they were evil." And then everything started to go downhill from there. The discussion that followed can be summarized as follows: "Of course we are Christians and we have more of a revelation today and, of course, we would never complain or murmur to God." There was even the suggestion that now that we are living in the New Covenant, there was really no need to study the Old Testament. Bad Old Testament, it speaks nothing relevant to us today.

Sure, after forty years of study, teaching and a few academic degrees focused on the Old Testament I will admit to some bias. But somebody has to speak out in defense of Old Testament and show its relevance. So let me first look at that word for *evil*. It is one of those *ra* words. This one ends with a "Hei." This evil is an evil of consumption. It is an evil that comes from letting natural desires consume you. It an evil that comes from being so consumed with the needs of the flesh that you fail to hear the voice of God. This evil congregation is one that focuses on the natural needs to the exclusion of addressing the spiritual needs. Of course such things are not relevant today, we are just too spiritually enlightened to have such a thing happen to us or the church. So let us move on.

The people of Israel tended to do a lot of murmuring. The word in Hebrew that is used here is *layan*, which basically means to *remain* or *stay*. It is a refusal to move forward out of lack of faith and receiving divine instruction. I would give this as more of a rendering rather than *worry* or *fretting*. Worry is nothing more than a lack of faith and refusal to receive divine instruction. Ouch! Do you feel the heat of relevance yet? I don't know about you but that one really burned me.

Finally, the word *bear* is not in Hebrew text. Actually, the literal rendering of this phrase is, "Until when will this evil congregation murmur to me?" In fact, let's look at this whole verse in a literal way: "Until when or how long will this congregation be so absorbed or focused on their natural needs that they will continue to refuse to move forward to the Promised Land. I heard the Children of Israel worry and fret and they are fretting against me." As Christians who belong to Jesus, when we worry or fret over our circumstances, we are fretting against Jesus.

I think before we pick up rocks and get ready to stone Israel, we should heed the warning of Jesus: "He who is without sin, let him cast the first stone". In all of my almost three score years of walking this earth, I have never known God to fail me. He is the one person who has never let me down, who has never rejected me. Yet, when I worry and fret over my circumstances, I am taking all those years of faithfulness and throwing them back in the face of God saying, "I don't trust you". Yeah, I, the guy who is always talking about seeking the heart of God can actually break His heart in the cruelest way. After years of proving Himself trustworthy, the moment my car breaks down, I begin to worry and fret. What? Am I the only unenlightened one here? Am I the only one who needs to examine the Old Testament to see my own reflection?

You see, Hebrew is a language of emotions. The words *al mati (until when)* are not an expression of anger, but a cry of the heart, a heart that has been broken. God is not expressing anger at the children of Israel for their murmurings, He is expressing a broken heart over having given so much to prove Himself trustworthy and then to be told he could not be trusted. Probably the most hurtful thing a spouse can say to one's beloved is "I don't trust you. I can't be intimate with you because you're not trustworthy enough."

If you are sitting back worrying and fretting over your circumstances, pause just for a moment, look beyond the natural and consider God's heart. Is it worth all that time and effort worrying and fretting over something that will not exist 50 years from now to break the heart of the God who has proven Himself worthy of your trust and the intimacy He longs to have with you?

DAY 7

Mercies (Chasad)

LAMENTATIONS 3:22-23: "IT IS the Lord's mercies that are not consumed, because His compassions fail not. They are new every morning, great is thy faithfulness."

"To never make a word I have not heard within my own heart." Edmond Rostand (Cyrano De Bergerac)

Edmond Rostand developed his character, Cyrano De Bergerac, to be the ultimate romantic poet and showed his heart when he declared that he swore he would "never make a word I have not heard in my own heart". I liken this to the Word of God as there is not a word in the Bible that does not originate from the heart of God.

The real beauty of Lamentations 3:22-23 is found in the word *mercies*. For me this is one of the most poetic words in the Bible coming from God's heart. This word is *chasad* and is spelled "Chet, Samek and Daleth". It means lovingkindness and mercy. But even with the position of the letters themselves, Chet, Samek, Daleth, cries out poetically the loving nature of the God we love in actually telling us what lovingkindness and mercy really is. For the letters and its position tell us that the lovingkindness of God is a portal to His heart and a joining of our hearts to His so that we may find peace and rest for our souls.

But is doesn't stop there for we learn in this verse that the mercies of God are never consumed. The word consume is *tamam*, which carries the idea of completion. The road to God's heart is never completed; there is no end. His heart is a well that will never run dry and when you plunge into that well of His heart, you can only fall deeper and deeper in one glorious glide to the depths of His being and never reach a bottom. The word *tamam* is spelled "Taw, Mem and Final Mem". The Taw in *tamam* suggests a cycle or process. This cycle will never end; it just keeps spiraling around. It is a cycle that carries a *Mem* and a final *mem*. The *Mem* represents the revealed Word of God and the final *Mem* represents the hidden knowledge of God. When we enter God's heart through His mercies that will never end we enter a revelation of His revealed Word and His hidden knowledge that will never end, we will spend eternity learning deeper and deeper things about God and never reach the bottom of that well. We see in the Book of Revelations that the angels are singing "Holy, Holy, Holy, to the Lord". They have done it for millions of years and never grow bored because they too are continually learning and experiencing something new about God. We only limit ourselves to God's revelation through our own experience with God.

Is it any wonder that Jeremiah wrote in verse 23: "They are new every morning . . ." The word *new* is *chadash*, which has a dual meaning of either brand new or renewed. As you journey through the heart of God, there is something new every morning and something within us is being renewed or restored. I have met many Christians who love Jesus with all their hearts, but they say they have grown bored with worship, they just don't feel the same sense of the presence of God they once did. Perhaps the problem is that God has called them to something new and yet they cling to something old. He is an infinite God and there are infinite ways to worship Him. We try reading books, or listening to CD's of other people's experience with God and try to duplicate that in our own lives. Yet, God may be trying to do something different in your own life. He may be trying to do something that is special for you and you alone. Maybe He is trying to make a Word that you, only you and you alone will hear within your own heart. God's Word is only limited by the amount of your heart that you are willing to share with Him.

We also learn that His compassions do not fail. The word *fail* has two possible roots, which could both be applicable to this verse. The first root word is *kala'*, which carries the idea of being confined and not allowed total expression. The second root word is *kalah*, which means to be destroyed. The word for compassion is *racham*, which is a very romantic word and not only means love but to "love tenderly". No Elvis Presley did not coin that term. A tender love is a ministering love. It is like a mother's love, which kisses the hurt to make it better. This is a love, which cannot be confined but must be allowed a total expression and on top of that, it can never be destroyed. This is the love that Paul spoke about in Romans 8. Nothing can separate us from the Love of God, which is in Christ Jesus. If we are not experiencing this tender love, His *racham*, then there is only one reason left as to why we don't and that reason lies within ourselves, within the amount of our own hearts that we are unwilling to share with God.

Jeremiah is telling us in these two verses that God has opened his whole heart up to us. There is nothing to separate us from His complete and total love. The only separation lies in the amount of our hearts that we do not give to Him. We may desire to give Him our whole hearts, but the amount of our hearts that we give Him depends upon the amount of trust we have in Him. If we have total and complete trust in His faithfulness, we can give Him our hearts totally and completely.

This may be why Jeremiah said: "Great is thy faithfulness". He knew God's faithfulness was great and thus he was able to give God his whole heart. The word *faithfulness* is from Hebrew root word *amen*. This word in its primitive meaning has the idea of a mother nursing a child. The total devotion of the mother giving herself to that child and the child's total dependence upon the mother is the picture being drawn for the word *faithfulness.*

I was reading in Jewish literature how the Bible does not speak of the God of Abraham, Isaac and Jacob, but speaks of the God of Abraham, the God of Isaac, and the God of Jacob. Each had to find their own place in God. They could not take the place of their fathers. They had to find God for themselves and let God reveal Himself in His own way that was special to each. So too, we do not seek the God of our pastor or favorite teacher, we seek our own personal God. Our God is one, but He is big; big enough for everyone to have a special, unique and personal place with Him. *Never make a word to God that you have not first heard in your own heart.*

DAY 8

Love (Chav, Racham)

JOHN 3:16: "FOR GOD so loved the world, that he gave his only begotten Son, that whosoever believeth in him should not perish, but have everlasting life."

John 21:20: "Then Peter, turning about, seeth the disciple whom Jesus loved following; which also leaned on his breast at supper, and said, Lord, which is he that betrayeth thee?"

We are all familiar with the three words in Greek expressing three levels of love, *Agape (unconditional love)*, *Phileo (brotherly love, friendship)* and *Eros (erotic love)*. Hebrew actually has four words for love, but they are not always translated as love. You have *Ahav (love)*, *Racham (tender mercies, Dodi (beloved as spousal love), and Ra'ah (brotherly love, or friendship)*. It would be wrong to try and make a parallel between the Greek words for love and Hebrew words as this would create a real problem in translation since *love* is at the very root and center of Scripture. I suppose we could say the closest to *Ahav* is Agape, *Ra'ah* is like *Phileo* and *Dodi* is like *Eros*. Yet this would not be accurate as *Ahav* is used in cases where *Agape* would not fit. *Ra'ah*, although rendered as friendship, is also rendered as shepherd and consuming passion and is often used by David to express his love for God, so it would be very inappropriate to consider *Ra'ah* equivalent to *Phileo* in many cases. *Dodi* is used by Solomon toward his beloved to express a sexual desire, but it does not carry the lustful, self-gratification of *Eros*.

There is a fourth word in Hebrew for love and that is *racham*, which is often expressed as a romantic love or rendered as *tender mercies*. It is rarely used in the Old Testament, but is frequently found in the Aramaic New Testament where it is spelled the same and sounds the same in Aramaic as it does in Hebrew.

In the Greek New Testament, we find that the word used for *love* in John 3:16 is *agape*. In the Peshitta or the Aramaic Bible it is the word *chav*, which is similar to Hebrew, word *ahav* and means *love*. However, in John 21:20 where we read about the disciple that Jesus *loved*, the Greek uses the word *agape*, but the Peshitta uses the Aramaic word *racham* which is identical to Hebrew word *racham*.

We know that Jesus and His disciples did not speak in Greek, but spoke in a Northern Old Galilean dialect of Aramaic. Aramaic is very difficult to translate into another language. I believe the original manuscripts of the Gospels were written in Aramaic and translated into Greek about twenty years later, but even if I am wrong and they were originally written in Greek, the writer would still have had to translate his words and those of Jesus directly from the Aramaic. We have Aramaic manuscripts that date earlier than our earliest Greek manuscripts, which were lost around 300 AD (oddly about the same time as Constantine). Still, even if Jesus and His disciples used two different Aramaic words for love, the writer and/or translator putting his words into Greek would have been stuck with only one possible word that would fit and that would be *agape*.

So when Jesus said that "God so loved the word" He used the Aramaic word *chav* but when speaking of the disciple that He *loved* we have the word *racham*. These are two entirely different words, both meaning *love*. The most logical conclusion is that we are dealing with two levels of love and thus this would suggest that he either loved the world more than His disciple or he loved this disciple more than the world. In other words, we face the old dilemma of Tommy Smother of the Smother brothers: "Mother always loved you best."

Is it true that God loves everyone, but does He have his favorites? Did He love Joseph more than me who is why he got to be a prime minister and I am just a bus driver? Did God love Moses more than Miriam and Aaron which is why He spoke face to face with Moses but not with his brother or sister?

Note that that John 21:20 does not say the disciple whom Jesus *loved*, but the disciple whom Jesus *loved following*. In the Greek and Aramaic it is more properly rendered as the disciple whom Jesus loved *who followed Him*. The world does not follow God, but this disciple did follow Jesus.

The key difference between the words *chav* which is used in John 3:16 as God loving the world and *racham* as used in John 21:20 of the disciple that Jesus loved is that *chav* is a love that is not necessarily returned. *Chav* is speaking of a love that flows from just one person, but that love may or may not be returned. For love to be completed, it must be returned.

Racham is a completed love. Love can be pretty lonely and painful if it is not returned. A young teenage girl can moon over some handsome dude who doesn't even know she is alive and feel depressed, sad and broken hearted, she can *chav*. But if that skinny little teenage guy looks into her eyes and says "I love you", she is immediately transported to cloud nine where birds sing and flowers look beautiful again. Love can exist if it is not returned, but it cannot sing until it is shared.

As a pastor, I performed many weddings. I have always been delighted to watch *chav* turn into *racham* as I spoke those words: "I now pronounce you husband and wife". At that moment the reality sets in on this couple, that they have now declared to the world that they love each other and are committing their lives to each other. In that declaration they know that they are truly *loved—racham*.

You see, God loves the word but the world does not love Him in return. It is when we love Him in return that His love is complete, it is when we love Him in return that he is able to rejoice over us with singing (Zephaniah 3:17). Salvation is not just about getting saved and going to heaven, it is about completing the love that God has for us, bringing that joy and celebration to the heart of God that heart that has been *mooning* over us for years, like that teenage girl and then to suddenly look into His eyes and say, "I love you'. Why do the angels rejoice over one sinner that repents? The same reason you cry at a wedding, you are rejoicing over seeing the joy of two people (not just one) who have found each other in love and share that love and return that love to each other. The angels rejoice for the same reason you read Jane Austen,

Elizabeth Barrett Browning, or Grace Livingstone Hill, they love a good romance where two people love each other.

It is not that God loves one person more than the other, He loves all equally. It is just that very few will love Him in return and complete His love, bringing Him the joy of His love, awakening Him in that love, and causing Him to sing with joy in that love.

You and I, simple little frail human beings, have the ability to bring joy to the God of the Universe by simply saying: "I love you". Have you told Him today that you love Him? Is God's love for you just *chav (one sided)?* Or is it *racham (completed, shared)?* Do you want to give the all mighty, all powerful God a thrill and make His day? Tell Him you love Him.

DAY 9

Lift Up (Nasah)

NUMBERS 6:26: "THE LORD lift up His countenance upon thee and give thee peace."

Lift up—Hebrew: *nasah*—to draw attention to

In a couple weeks we will be holding a conference in Terra Haute, Indiana. One thing I am hoping to accomplish in this conference is to teach the people attending how to study the Word of God with their hearts. This verse in Numbers might be a good starting point for it is a verse we hear often in a benediction. Yet we often hear and understand it with our minds, but rarely do we seek to understand it with our hearts. When we hear this verse with our hearts, there can be many different renderings, yea hundreds of renderings, but only one that is specific to you personally. For God is speaking to you personally in this verse and Hebrew is such an ambiguous language that there is room for God to speak many different things to different people. He is an infinite God and He has infinite ways of speaking His love to us. Neither I, nor any other teacher or preacher can tell you what God is saying to you personally in this verse, you must experience it, feel it and live it to know what it means.

Let me just give you a little nudge in this direction by pointing out that the word rendered as *lift up* in Hebrew is *nasah* and really means *to draw attention to* and you could read this as "May the Lord draw our attention to his countenance." But thanks to the ambiguous nature of Hebrew language, there are many different ways to render or understand this verse, at least when you seek to understand it from your heart and the heart of God rather than just your mind.

In oriental culture, a mere peasant or servant was not permitted to look a king in the eye. When in the presence of the king one must look down and not at his face. This is not only to show respect, but to keep the servants from becoming too familiar with the king. It was a way of exercising control, keeping a person in his place so to speak. Also, your facial expressions and your eyes reveal a lot about you. One can see weakness, or maybe favor or lack of favor by looking into someone's eyes. Without looking into the kings face, one could never know what the king was feeling. Yet, our King of all Kings is *drawing our attention to His countenance*. He wants His people to see what He is feeling. Why would our Lord want to draw our attention to His countenance? Perhaps it is to see the love lights in His eyes.

If you love your Savior with all your heart and knowing He loves you with all His heart you will understand the picture being drawn in this verse. It is the picture of two lovers making eye contact and in just that once glance you fall into nothingness, rejoicing in the presence of love. In the presence of true love all pain and suffering seems to vanish. Yesterday my study partner was suffering from a toothache. But she attended a school play that her nephew was in anyways and spent a little time with him after the play. She claimed that the toothache went away when she was with her nephew (or surrounded by his love).

The word *countenance is* the word *pani* in Hebrew and is often rendered as *presence.* When one is in love nothing else matters in the world, all the pain and suffering seems to vanish. Heck even a dog or cat that expresses love to you seems to take away even physical pain and indeed such animals are often used for therapeutic reasons.

In Jewish literature there is the story of man of some influence who received many expensive gifts from various people, many who were seeking his favor because of His status. Yet, one day he received a very small inexpensive gift from the king. This gift became his prized possession, because it was a gift from his king. Jews always say a prayer or blessing after a meal, not just before a meal like we do. They give this blessing regardless of how much or how little food they have, for whatever they have, no matter how little, comes from their king and just the fact that it comes from their king they prize that little gift.

No matter how small or great our portion is in this life, we all have one thing equal and in common and that is that God will offer his presence and peace to all on an equal basis. That should be enough. The mere fact that our King will allow us to look upon His face and see the love lights in His eyes, is all the reward we should ever need.

The next time your priest or pastor quotes this verse in a benediction, hear it with your heart and not with your mind, for then you may just hear the words: "May the Lord draw attention to his loving presence" or you might hear "May the

Lord draw attention to the love lights in His eyes" or you may hear something else that brings you peace for you see, mere words do not a translation make. It is also the expression of the love between you and your Savior that will render the translation that is correct for you and you alone.

DAY 10

Prosper (Salach)

GENESIS 39:3 "AND HIS master saw that the Lord was with him and the Lord made all that he did to prosper in his hand."

Prosper: Hebrew—Salach: prosper, moving forward, and making accomplishments.

"Now I lay me down to rest, for tomorrow comes yet another test. If I die before I wake, that is at least one more test I need not take." *My bedtime prayer.*

Joseph and I have many things in common but one thing we don't have in common is that the Lord does not make all that I do to prosper in my hand. However, I decided to look at this verse anyways.

There are a few things in this verse that causes one to stop and ponder. First, Potiphar saw that the Lord was with Joseph. In Hebrew the word used for Lord is the word Jehovah or *YHVH*. What did an Egyptian official know about the Hebrew God? How did he know it was God making everything to prosper? And what is this prosperity business anyways? To get beaten by one's brothers, sold into slavery, later accused of a rape he did not commit and getting thrown into prison does not sound prosperous to me.

The word *prosper* in Hebrew is *salach*. This word does not mean to prosper as we would interpret *prosper* in our culture, i.e., material possessions. Here the word *prosper* has the idea of moving forward, making progress. This is in a hiphal form not a piel form so it would not have the idea of gain, but more of the idea of just getting things accomplised. The word is spelled "Sade, Lamed, Chet" so it would have the idea of accomplishing things humbly, prayerfully, and in unity with God. This may be what caught Potiphar's attention. Joseph was not motivated like the other slaves. Joseph went about his work accomplishing his tasks for something or someone much higher than Potiphar and Potiphar saw this. Prosperity here has to do with performing a task, even an earthly task for an earthly boss as if we are serving God and not man. Prosperity or *salach* is to do any job as unto God humbly, prayerfully and in unity with Him.

That really does not answer the question as to how Potiphar knew it was God Jehovah? I checked through Jewish literature and found something interesting. The words "with him" are translated from the Hebrew word *ethu*. The ancient rabbis saw the *eth* as a sign of the direct object and the *hu'* as a pronoun. In other words it would be literally rendered: "Potiphar saw that the Lord is Joseph". That doesn't make much sense until you consider that the word *saw* is *ra'ah* which could mean seeing in a spiritual sense as well as a natural sense. I am not sure of a proper rendering but I do know what this verse is saying. When Potiphar saw Joseph, he saw God Jehovah. There is an old saying: "You are the only Jesus people will ever see."

A seventeenth century rabbi, Rabbi Yisroel Ben Eliezer. rendered the passage this way: "And his master saw that the name of God was always upon his lips". This is what caught Potiphar's attention, he saw a man who always performed his tasks humbly, prayerfully and in unity with God always with the name of God upon his lips. When he saw Joseph, he saw God.

The greatest prosperity would be for someone to say, "I see Jesus in your face and hear Him upon your lips". To myself as with any believer that would mean more than winning the mega lottery.

DAY 11

Protective Cover (Yasak)

PSALMS 91:4: "HE SHALL cover thee with feathers and under his wings shalt thou trust. His truth shall be thy shield and buckler."

C.S. Lewis once commented that if we were to take Psalms 91 literally, it would be bad for the church. To take this literally would mean that nothing bad will ever happen to us as long as we are sheltered under His wings. One would never experience relationship problems, financial problems, health problems etc. Word gets out churches would be filled with people all attending church for the wrong reasons.

The word *cover* is *yasak*. There are three possible root words from which this word is derived. One could be *suk* which is a covering from an anointing, the other could be *nasak* which is a covering from just pouring something over one's head, like pouring syrup over a waffle. The third and most commonly accepted root word is *sukok*. This is the same word used in Job for *hedge* when the enemy accused God of putting a *hedge* around Job.

This points to that protective covering that he places around the believer like the one that He put around Israel.

Here that protective hedge is pictured as feathers. The word *feathers* is *abavar*. The primitive meaning is strength and might that comes from returning to one's core values. Thus, the picture of being covered by His feathers is more of empowerment that comes from returning to God's basic principles rather than one of protection.

"Under his wings we will trust". The word *wings* is *kaneph* which has the idea of an extreme or being removed to a distant place. Wings come from that idea as they are able to carry a bird to places that man cannot go. The picture is indeed one of protection, but a protection that comes when you allow God to carry you to places that he so chooses to take you. You may not know where His is taking you. You are simply to trust in Him as He carries you to His destination. The word *trust* is *chasach* which is the idea of a refuge. In a refuge you feel safe and confident. This is the trust you find in Him, a feeling of confidence that you are in a safe place. The journey he has you on is a safe one where He is with you every moment.

The key idea to this empowerment and protection lies in being obedient to his will and going where he takes you. Once the children of Israel stopped moving they were frozen in their tracks through fear and worry. The protective covering of God was lifted and the enemy was able to come in for an attack.

It is this last line that strikes interest. His truth is a shield. Truth here is *aman* which is a steadfastness or faithfulness. His faithfulness and steadfastness is our shield. The word used for shield is *sanah* which comes from the idea of thorns, sharpness and protection. His faithfulness is our *buckler*. The word for buckler is *sacher*, which is the word used for wealth, profit or the seat of commerce. His faithfulness is our wealth and profit.

What I am seeing in this is not so much a protection in the natural as more an eternal protection. This is an assurance that we will always prosper spiritually when we are obedient to God. When we are obedient to Him, He will empower us; He will take us where he wants us to go. I don't see Him necessarily promising us an easy journey, just a journey where He is always with us.

As the children of Israel journeyed to the promise land, it was not an easy journey, they had to fight some battles, they had to face the elements, but they always had the protective covering of God. As long as they were obedient to Him, they were covered in His feathers and trusted, or found a safe place under His wings. It was God's faithfulness that protected them and carried them into the Promised Land. This is the same faithfulness that will carry us through this journey in life.

Day 12

Purpose (Chapats)

ECCLESIASTES 3:1: TO EVERYTHING there is a season, and a time to every purpose under the heaven:

I was taught in my theology classes that Ecclesiastes 3:1-8 was a quodlebet. A quodlbet is a theological or philosophical point of view which is presented for debate or argumentation. You have seven verses with each containing two pairs of opposites to support the writers thesis found in verse one, "to everything there is a season". The writer is following the theme of Ecclesiastes which is to express the brevity and/or futility of life.

There are a total of fourteen pairs of opposites that are contrasted to show that God has appointed or determined the appropriate moment or time and we as human beings cannot control the moments or purposes fixed by God.

The key to understanding these eight verses is to understand the first verse where the writer presents his thesis and it would be helpful to zero in on the key word where the writer builds his argument. I believe that key word is the word *purpose*.

The first words in this verse in Hebrew are curious: *lakol zeman ve'ith*. Literally this means *to all the old men and seasons*. Actually, the noun form of *zeman* is *beard* where we get the idea of an old man or the process of aging. The word *seasons* is Hebrew word *ve'ith* which comes from the root word *'adah* in a literal sense means *seasons* but is rooted in the idea of pass by, to abolish or put away. Oddly, it has a secondary meaning of ornament, as in something which is beautiful for only a short period of time. Lately, we have been seeing trees blossom. They are very beautiful when they blossom, but it is only temporary and already it is passing.

I recently discovered a little word called "images" on the menu bar of Google. When I clicked on it under the name of my favorite movie and TV stars of the sixties and seventies, I saw photos of this star today. I am amazed as I see photos of these stars today, they are old. The handsome men I envied as a child or the women I thought were so beautiful are now all showing the signs of wear and tear of age. Like one preacher said, your parents will catch up with you—Father Time and Mother Nature. As I drive our seniors to their medical appointments during the week, one common question I always get is, "Why do we have to grow old". Solomon asked the same question in the Book of Ecclesiastes.

The literal translation of verse 3:1 is: *To all the old men and the passing of time there is a purpose under heaven*. Just as the natural world goes through its seasons, so too is man put on this earth to age and go through his seasons. He has his moments of beauty but like the blooming flowers which quickly fades, so too does man go through a period of blooming and then fads away. God has a purpose in all this.

The age old question: "Why do we grow old?" is argued in the following verses, but ultimately the answer is that God has a *purpose*.

Hence the key to understanding this is to understand this word *purpose*. The word in Hebrew is *chapats*. If that word sounds familiar to some of my students, it should; it is the word that is commonly rendered as *delight, or to take pleasure in.* In a noun form it is used as precious stones or precious things. In other words the literally rendering of this verse is: *To all the old men and the passing of time there is preciousness under heaven.*

I have read many scholarly works which question the role of the Book of Ecclesiastes in the canon because it is such a depressing book filled with hopelessness and despair. It is pure existentialism straight out of Albert Camus.

Yet, if you look at the undercurrent of this book, you find that what Solomon is teaching is that without the hope of eternity, without God, the world and our existence is indeed meaningless. However, if we were created by a God for His pleasure, to complete His circle of love then the only hope of meaning in our existence is to bring pleasure to this God, our creator.

That is Solomon's quodlibet; his philosophical argument is that God has created a time for mourning and a time for laughing for without the contrast of laughter to mourning we could not experience the full joy of laughing. Without the problems of life, God would not have the opportunity to show His love by resolving these problems. Without sorrow, God could not enjoy the opportunity to bring us joy.

Here is what is important. Note that Solomon never mentions God in all this. He is not saying that God is the author of our sorrow and suffering. Solomon is only arguing that God is an opportunist. He is the knight in shining armor looking for the dragon to slay and we in our fallible, bumbling and sinful way are constantly creating and giving Him the dragons to slay to win our hand as His fair maidens.

Day 13
Persecution (Radaph)

Psalms 23:6: "Surely goodness and mercy shall follow me all the days of my life and I will dwell in the house of the Lord forever."

Mark 10:30: "But he shall receive an hundredfold now in this time, houses, and brethren, and sisters, and mothers, and children, and lands, with persecutions; and in the world to come eternal life."

I was reading the Book of Mark this morning in my Peshitta (Aramaic Bible) and I ran across a curious word in the Aramaic. It is the word *reduphya*, which being interpreted means *persecutions*. This word comes from the root word *radaph*, which is identical to the Hebrew word *radaph* and is the same word used in Psalms 23:6 where it is rendered as *follow*.

I quickly checked my Greek New Testament and the word used for *persecution* is *digmon* from the root word *diko*. This is a good, solid, no nonsense straight forward word meaning persecution.

The word *radaph (follow, persecute)* is a common Semitic word found in other Semitic languages. I found the word in both the Akkadian and Ugaritic language as well. It's most common use is *persecution*. The idea of *follow* grew out of the fact that this a persecution that is a nagging type of persecution. It is not a one-time bop on the head for standing up for some cause. This is the persecution of a nagging boss who is always pointing out your faults. It is a chronic affliction like a cold that follows you around causing you to cough, sneeze, and making you feel chilled and feverish, all constant reminders that you have a cold.

Sometimes we even say that our boss is *persecuting* us or that our cold is *persecuting* us. This is the intent in both Mark 10:30 and Psalms 23:6. When you examine this word letter by letter you begin to see just what the nature of this persecution is. The word is spelled Resh, Daleth, Pei. The Resh tells us that this persecution comes from someone who is continually being judgmental and self-righteous. Do you know anyone who just wears you down with their continual accusations of all your faults while they self-righteously hold themselves up as someone who has overcome or who are above such faults? Such a persecutor will drive you insane with the next letter, the shadow of the Daleth which is false humility. Of course it is the last letter, the Pei, which finally brings you down, the shadow of the Pei is the constant negative talk, telling you how rotten and no good you are.

For me, David's use of the word *radaph* in Psalm 23:6 has staggering implications. David is not saying that goodness and mercy are following him around, stroking him, soothing him. Goodness and mercy are persecuting him. The word *goodness* in Hebrew is *tov* which means to be in harmony with God. The word *mercy* is *chasad*. Oddly, this word is identical to the Aramaic word *chasad,* which means to bring shame, reproach and disgrace upon someone. Indeed in extra Biblical literature *chasad,* as used in Hebrew, is also used on occasion to express the idea of bringing shame, reproach and disgrace upon someone. The idea of bringing this shame, reproach and disgrace upon someone is that when faced with true *mercy* you are made more aware of your offense because you are not being punished for your crime. You feel shame, reproach and disgrace because you know you are guilty and deserve to be punished and here the person you offended forgives you. That is the message of the cross. We look upon Jesus suffering for our sins on the cross and knowing that we will not have to suffer for our sins and this mercy fills us with reproach and disgrace for our sins. Our sins caused the Jesus we love to suffer and to bring suffering upon someone you truly love only brings you shame, disgrace, and reproach.

Yes, goodness and mercy are a good thing but not in the sense we think. It is a good thing that it follows us around all our lives, persecuting us, bringing us shame, reproach and disgrace for our sins. It brings us such shame, reproach and disgrace that we do not want to sin. Sin is just not worth all the shame, reproach and disgrace.

Of course we do not want to sin because we will die and go to hell. Right? I think David did not want to sin because he knew right behind him was goodness (his harmonious life with God) and mercy (God's lovingkindness and suffering for his sins) that kept nagging at him: "David, shame on you, shame, look how you hurt the God you love, look how God loves you so much He forgives you and yet you continue to wound his heart, shame on you."

As I draw closer to the heart of God I find I begin to love Him more and more. The more I love Him the more I find my two persecutors (Goodness and Mercy) following me around, nagging me saying, "Oh, so you are going to watch that movie when you promised to spend time with the God you love, shame on you, He is looking forward to that time with you, but in your selfishness, wanting to please your own gizzard, you've wounded His heart. Shame, shame. You want to sin then go ahead, go ahead, we're only Goodness and Mercy for crying out loud, don't let us stand in your way. Go; Go have you pleasant little time away from God." Goodness and Mercy will just keep nagging me until I finally cry out, "Alright, already, where's my Hebrew Bible." Sin and go to hell? Heck, Goodness and Mercy makes the very thought of sinning hell itself.

Day 14

Continually Serve (Palak)

Daniel 6:16: "The king spake and said unto Daniel: "Thy God whom thou serves continually, He will deliver you."

In researching my doctoral dissertation I came across something very curious which may serve to shed some light on King Darius's statement to Daniel that God would deliver him from the lion's den. This portion of the Book of Daniel was written in Aramaic which is very difficult to translate into another language. There are many variations we can use in arriving at an equivalent word in the English language for many Aramaic words. The writer uses a strange word for *serve*. The word in Aramaic is *palak* which in a noun form means a *millstone*. In its verbal form it means to *grind or cut up into pieces*. It is possible that what King Darius is referring to is Daniel's fanaticism, *the God that you have ground yourself up into.*

Then he adds the noun *bor* which has the prefix *Beth* which is the preposition for *on or in* and the suffix *Aleph* which is a definite article *the*. It means a *circle or to dwell within the circle*. What King Darius could possibly be referencing is that Daniel has allowed God to grind him up into his little circle that there was no hope of his seeing any other way. There was just no possible way that Daniel would serve any other God.

But then he adds something very enlightening. He says that *God will deliver him*. The Aramaic word used here is *shazav* which means to rescue or deliver, but it is a deliverance made out of love and affection. King Darius is saying that if your God loves you so much, He will not let you suffer this fate. Oh, but there is more embedded in this word. It is in a Peil Imperfect form. Hebrew does not have a reflexive form for the Piel stem, but Aramaic does. The Peil is a combination Piel (Intensive) and Hithapael (reflexive). What King Darius is saying, if we are true to the grammatical use for this word, is: "The God that you have totally committed yourself to will deliver you to protect Himself". In others, it would be a major embarrassment to God if he does not rescue you from these lions.

Now we need to examine just why the lions are so important here. I found a picture of an ancient artifact that shows King Darius's son Artaxeres II standing before the figure of the goddess Anahita riding on a lion. Anahita is the Sun God of ancient Persia and the protector of Persia. Mithras, or the lion is the symbol of the Persian deity depicting strength and unity. That unity was very important as the Persian Empire was made up of many conquered nations, but each conquered nation shared in the governmental structure of the Persian Empire, hence we have Daniel as one of its three presidents who was also a prince of the Judean Empire. This lion symbolized the strength of the Persian Empire and it is that strength that would keep the Empire united with the conquered nations. It was recognized that in unity there was strength and power. Yet to be unified all had to ascribe to one primary god. In this case the goddess Anahita was elected. This is why we see her pictured riding on the lion.

If anyone violated or placed another god above Anahita, they would have to face the wrath of the lions and hence the lion's den was kept for that very reason. The real lions were kept to punish anyone who desecrated the authority of the reigning god or goddess. That is why it was so easy to set Daniel up and get King Darius to sign the proclamation that no one could worship any god other than Anahita.

This was not just a battle in the physical realm but in the spiritual realm as well. If Daniel survived the lion's den, then the whole religious order, if not governmental structure of the kingdom would be threatened. This is why King Darius ordered everyone to worship Jehovah. The elite of the kingdom saw God Jehovah go toe to toe with the sun god Anahita and it wasn't even a close call. As they threw Daniel into the lion's den, the angel shut the mouths of the lions. There must have been a lot of lions in there because the servants of Anahita were thrown in next and they with their families numbered almost three hundred and the Bible says they were devoured before they even hit the ground. Once in the lion's den it is very possible Daniel, who understood the secrets of God, practiced a little *yaredu (dominion)* and those lions became nothing more than house cats.

I read a story in Jewish literature about a Jewish community that bordered another pagan community. Lions would often come into the pagan community and attack its citizens but never bothered anyone from the Jewish community. The leaders of the pagan community noticed this and called the Jewish leaders to find out why the lions never attacked. The Jewish leaders came and taught the pagan leaders the secrets of *yaredu* and the lions never bothered anyone anymore. Whether Daniel practiced *yaredu* or not, we do know one thing for certain: King Darius knew that Daniel had a personal relationship with the God of the universe and not only that this God would protect Daniel because this God Jehovah loved Daniel, which is a whole lot more than you can say for Anahita. Apparently she turned out to be a no show when it came time to put her servants to the lions.

DAY 15

Cleaveth (Davak)

PSALMS 119:25: "MY SOUL cleaveth unto the dust, quicken thou me according to thy word."

"In times of change, learners inherit the earth, while the learned find themselves beautifully equipped to deal with a world that no longer exists."—Eric Hoffer

Most Christian commentators interpret the phrase; "My soul cleaveth unto the dust" as an expression of dying. However, the Jewish sages bring out something very interesting about that word *cleave*. In Hebrew the word is *davak* which means *to cleave* but it also means to *follow closely*. Now, of course, in our Western thinking, if we render the word as *cleave* then we certainly cannot render it as *follow*. Yet, we must not forget that this is poetry and there are certain play on words that writers can and do make.

There was an ancient belief that your soul passes through your feet. It was believed that when a master teacher walked, he left trances of his wisdom and knowledge in his footprints. His followers would seek to step in the footprints of their master in hopes that they would absorb some of that knowledge that was left behind. That is where the expression "walking in his footsteps" comes from. Sometimes they would roll in the dust that their master would kick up in hopes of capturing some of that wisdom and knowledge. The sages feel that David may be making an allusion to this picture. David is putting himself in the position a disciple or learner to his master—God Jehovah. Thus his soul is clinging or following the dust that God leaves, hoping to gain just a trance of Godly wisdom and knowledge.

The word *cleave* is spelled Daleth, Beth, Qof. Ancient Jewish teachings on this word tells that the Daleth is a doorway to the Beth or heart of God and that the Qof tell us that sacrifice is the doorway to come closer to the divine. Jesus made it clear that there is only one sacrifice that will bring us closer to God and that is His own sacrifice of his life on the cross. The word for *dust* is *'aphar* which is the word for *dust or dirt* and is the same word used for what God formed man out of and what man will return to. The word *aphar* is sometimes used for natural man. Now I do agree with the Christian commentators that this is an expression of death. That being the case, we seem to have a nice little packaged expression of the Messiah Jesus coming to earth in human form to sacrifice his life so that man can draw close to God and know His heart.

This is followed by the expression "quicken me according to your word." The word *quicken* is *chani* from the root word *chi* which is *life*. David is saying: "Bring me life according to your word." Odd, the words *according to* are not found in Hebrew text. That is drawn from the *Kap* in front of the word *devar*. It is more appropriately rendered: "like your word". *Devar* is a divine *word* similar to the Greek word *rhema*. Did not Jesus say, "I am the Word of life". Believe what you want but I believe buried deep within the esoteric nature of Hebrew we see not only a picture of Jesus but also a prophecy of His coming.

Let's back up and look at this meaning found under the surface. Actually, I see two possible meanings here that are not apparent in a first reading. The first is the Christian understanding that David is about to die and he is asking God to quicken or revive his life according to His word.

Our first thought, of course, is that the word is the Bible. Yet, the only Bible David had was the Torah, the first five books of the Bible. When David refers to the Torah, he calls it that. The word used here is *davar* and not *torah* which is a *divine spoken word*. David's life is restored by the divine spoken word of God.

There is yet another picture here and that is following the Jewish approach and seeing this matter of "clinging to the dust" as a search for the wisdom and knowledge of God. David is saying that he is rolling in the dust of God, or that he is seeking a personal Word from God.

People will purchase books, CD's, listen to radio and TV teachers, and travel to distant places to attend workshops and seminars, hoping to get a *Word* from God. There is nothing terribly wrong with this. The learned can give us some wonderful words that we can all use, except like David, there does come a time when you need to get your own *Word* from God. That means seeking and searching for Him with all your heart, soul and might, not just listening to a CD. As the American Longshoreman philosopher Eric Hoffer said, "In times of change it is the learner who inherits the earth, not the learned." The words of the learned are good, but during times of personal change, like David, we need to get our own personal word from God. There are times we need, like David, to roll in the dust of God and not the dust of man.

DAY 16

Satyrs (Se'irim)

ISAIAH 13:21-22: "BUT WILD beasts of the desert shall lie there; and their houses shall be full of doleful creatures; and owls shall dwell there, and satyrs shall dance there. The hyenas shall cry in its towers, and jackals in their pleasant palaces: her time is near, and her days shall not be prolonged"

I drive a bus for senior citizens and the disabled, taking them to their medical appointments. I recently drove one elderly lady who hails from the Deep South with a dirt water accent and all. From the time she got on my bus to the time she got off she delighted us with all her backwoods stories. She told this one story: "My daddy was preacher, a Baptist preacher, he'd baptize anyone, didn't care if you were Catholic or Presbyterian, he'd baptize ya. He even tried to baptize the dog. The ole dog, he didn't like it much, he fought 'em. The deacon, he said, 'Why you tryin' to baptize that poor ole dog, he didn't do nutin' wrong.' But my daddy he said, 'Ya don't know that, ya just gotta be sure.' Yep, that's what my daddy always said, 'Ya gotta be sure.'"

Well, we all know animals are not in need of redemption or repentance as they do not have a free will and they cannot sin. Yet, I have heard many Christians attribute demonic activity on some poor creatures for no other reason than the fact that they are ugly or sinister looking like owls, ravens, goats etc. I mean if the demons are going to possess an animal why choose the ugly ones, why not the beautiful ones. After all the chief demon himself is called an angel of light and was the most beautiful creature in the garden. If you are going to deceive someone why make it so obvious and dress him up as a toad?

Others will draw on passages of Scripture such as Isaiah 13:21-22 and say: "Lookie here, the owl is placed right up there with a satyr, a demonic creature, he too must be demonic by association." Poor old owl, he did nothing wrong but scare the living pudding out of you one night by giving an innocent hoot, it ain't his fault. Yet, we categorize animals into Godly creatures and satanic creatures while paradoxically all animals are created by God Himself.

Isaiah 13:21-22 is a very curious passage and one that shows that even our best language experts, linguist and students of ancient languages still have much more to learn about our ancient Semitic languages.

One hundred and eighty years before the fall of Babylon we have Isaiah prophesying not only of its destruction but how desolate the city will be after the destruction. It will be so desolate that wild animals will dwell in the city rather than human beings. Isaiah list six types of animals that will live and possess the ruined city. You have *tsiyim* (wild beast of the deserts), *'ochim* (doleful creatures), *benoth ya'enah* (owls), *se'irim* (satyrs), *iyim* (hyenas) *and tanim* (jackals).

Here is the rub, no one can say for certain what these animals really are. *Tsiyim* (wild beast of the deserts) have been rendered as everything from lions to porcupines. 'Ochim (doleful creatures) have been rendered as hyenas, jackals and owls. The simple fact is, translators can only guess as to the identity of these animals. No one knows for sure what animals Isaiah is referring to. Now you couple that with the fact that the ancients did not break down the animal kingdom into specifics like we do. Therefore a hyena, jackal and fox were all the same animals to the ancients. A wolf, dog and even a hyena were still all considered dogs. Actually, each of these names only describes the animal, it doesn't really name the specific breed of the animal. The animals listed are "deserts creature, howling creatures, doleful creatures, creatures of the night and desert howlers". These descriptions fit any number of animals and for us to really specify whether the animal is a fox, jackal or hyena, would be impossible as not even the ancients knew for sure. If I am going to say one animal is demonic rather than another then Sparky, my neighbor's pit bull, would be just as demonically possessed as a jackal (maybe he is).

There is one curious animal that is mentioned, that is the *satyr*. It is this rendering that has led many of our ultra conservative Bible teachers to assume these animals are all demonic as the satyr is associated with a demonic creature. Actually, a satyr was a minor deity from Greek mythology, not Babylonian mythology. The satyr was a male companion to Pan (god of wild sheep and goats) and Dionysus (god of wine and winemaking). A satyr was half goat and half man and all were associated with eroticism and fertility. They are pictured as always dancing, symbolizing hedonistic behavior in the style of the *Great Gatsby*.

The word in Hebrew which is rendered as *satyr* is *se'irim*, which simply means *to be hairy*. Mountain and wild goats were hairy and before long *se'irim* became associated with goats. If you were looking for a Hebrew word to put to a *satyr*, *se'irim* would be a logical choice. Keep in mind that the *satyr* is a god of Greek mythology and we are dealing with Babylon here and a prophet who lived hundreds of years before Greek mythology.

I would avoid using the rending of *se'irim* as *satyr* only because it could prove very misleading to teachers looking for a platform and drawing a conclusion that all the animals associated with a *se'irm* are demonic. Come on, let's give the poor creatures a break. I am not saying that demons cannot possess animals, I am only saying that we should not persecute these poor creatures for something their daddies did long ago. A goat can't help it if he were born a goat.

So why mention all these creatures and associate them with the destruction of Babylon? One clue might be found in the diary of a Benjamin Tudelensis, a sixteenth century explorer who came upon the ruins of Babylon. In his diary he said he would not approach the city because of all the dangerous creatures such as jackals, wolves, and poisonous snakes that dwelled there. Each one of these creatures mentioned in Isaiah 13:21-21 can be rendered as a creature which possesses a threat to mankind. Perhaps the prophet was saying that the even the most powerful armies could not protect the city from intrusion but God can send his own creation of innocent animals that will turn many away.

Perhaps the prophet is saying that God can take the dwellings of the mighty and turn them over to his own creation if He so wishes. There are any number of lessons we can draw from this, so maybe we should give the owl a break. Just because he happens to be nocturnal and scare the bejeebers out of you by making a spooky sound it does not mean we need to throw rocks at him. He is just as much a creation of God as Sparky my neighbor's pit bull (although sometimes I do wonder about Sparky).

Day 17

Follow Hard (Devekah)

Psalms 63:8: "My soul follow hard after you, your right hand upholds me."

I am having a hard time (that's a pun) reconciling coincidences as just beating out the odds or as a message from God. For instance, this morning I was reading about rabbis who entered a state of *devekut* during prayer. As I continue on my journey to discover the heart of God, I am quite fascinated with the Jewish sage's devotion to prayer as a means to achieve a oneness with God. There is a record of one rabbi who would roll on the floor while praying: "I don't want to enter the Garden of Eden, I don't want to enter the kingdom of God, I just want God." There is another account of a rabbi who would enter into such a deep prayer that he would begin to ask God to let him remain with him forever. One day he was in such a deep state of prayer or *devekut* that it frightened the family. The son began to shake his father to cause him to stop praying but he could not do it. The father suddenly collapsed into his son's arms and died. There is a record of more than one rabbi who passed from this life to the next in such a deep state of prayer or *devekut* that they called it the "kiss of God."

Now I am not talking about such an extreme devotion to prayer, but yet there is something in this state of prayer call *devekut* that makes me wonder if I am just scratching the surface with my own personal poor excuse for prayer. Anyways, I figured that would be a topic I would research later. But, oddly enough, later was really right now. Was it just one of those coincidences or is it God trying to teach me something?

My soul was feeling distressed this morning and I figured it was time I moved from reading about man's experience to what God is teaching, and to spend some time in His Word. When my soul is feeling troubled I often find myself drawn to the Psalms. I opened my Hebrew Bible and just randomly picked out Psalms 63: I began reading and found myself getting little bored as this Psalm was not really addressing my need. I was just about to move to another Psalm when I read verse 8 and there it was: "Devekah nepeshi acherika" The KJV translates this as "my soul follows hard after you." Some translations render this as "My soul clings to you." The word for "follows hard' or "clings" is (you guessed it) "devek." *Devek* or devekut simply means to *cling to*. In Modern Hebrew it is the word for glue. The Jewish sages teach that it means a gateway to the heart of God through holiness and sanctification. It looks like King David also practiced devekut. Maybe it was not a *practice* so much as a way of life or just a natural state as it is for two lovers who hold hands, hug, kiss and share an intimacy. They do not practice *intimacy*, they just simply live it, it is something that is just a normal part of their relationship.

In the context of this Psalm, David is so hungry for God that his soul has entered a state of *devekut* or clinging (hugging) God. One Jewish writer describes a prayer of *devekut* as not praying anything for yourself, but seeking only to bring pleasure to God. It is a state of total humility. Hebrew word for humility does not mean thinking little of yourself. The idea of humility in Hebrew is to lose all sense of yourself in the presence of God. It is in this state of humility that one enters a devekut.

My first thought, of course, is what I have been taught in my good Baptist tradition that one must never enter into such a deep meditative state. Such a thing is dangerous since the enemy can enter. The old devil can push God aside and say: "No you don't either, he is mine, I am going to take advantage of this moment." Sort of like a man and woman on their honeymoon about to have an intimate moment when an old girl friend arrives and says: "Ok, I'll take over from here." That is not about to happen unless, of course, the old boy desires her more than his new wife. Perhaps this is why David says that the "right hand of God sustains me." The right hand of God represents God's power. David is saying that even if he enters a state of *devekut* with God and loses all sense of self, the power of God will sustain him.

Here's the clincher, you do not need to enter a trance like state to be in *devekut. Devekut* is simply losing all sense of self. There is an old saying: "Looking out for No. 1." In this case that No. 1 is "Aleph" or God.

I have been reading a book about a woman named Heidi Bakker who appears to be living in a constant state of *devekut*. She is not living in a trance, but again she is not living a normal life. You don't establish 5,000 churches in third world nations and take care of thousands of orphans living in a trance. But at the same time, she is living in a state of losing one's sense of self, and as a result she has done some things which seem pretty foolish in the natural. Yet, by living in this state of clinging to God, being glued to Him, in constant communion with Him, the Lord has sustained her with His right hand or His power.

So as I approach my trials today, I learn that they are only trials when I have a sense of self. But if I enter that state of *devekut* and lose that sense of self, the trials are no longer trials but simply part of the journey of life I am taking with God by my side.

Day 18

Follow ('Azal or 'Etha)

JOHN 1:40: "ONE OF the two which heard John *speak*, and *followed* him, was Andrew, Simon Peter's brother"

John 1:43: "The day following Jesus went forth into Galilee, and found Philip, and said unto him, "*Follow* me.""

Andrew *followed* Jesus and Jesus asked Philip to *follow* Him. In the Greek text the same word is used which is *akoloutheo*, it means what we expect *follow* to mean, that is to *follow, accompany or to attend to someone.*

In the Old Galilean Aramaic dialect, which Jesus spoke, however, we find that there are two different words used. We learn Peter *followed* Jesus in verse 40 and the Aramaic word that is used is '*azal* which means to follow. 'Azal however is often used in the Old Galilean as an idiomatic expression with a military idea which is to follow someone to the death. When the Bible says that the disciples were following Jesus, they were doing more than just *akoloutheo* or simply traveling with Jesus, they were committed to following Jesus even at the cost of their own lives.

Now this may not seem too dramatic when you consider the fact that they had no police force at all in those days and the only protection were the Roman soldiers who occupied the land. No man would travel from one town to the next alone, he would be prey to any number of bandits. As the old saying goes, "there is safety in numbers." We learn that Peter carried a sword which he used to chop off the ear of a soldier. Carrying a weapon was not uncommon for those who traveled from town to town; they would often carry weapons to protect themselves and others from bandits that would attack. In Luke 10:4 Jesus instructed his disciples to "*Carry neither purse, nor scrip, nor shoes: and salute no man by the way.*" If we were to put this in a modern context we would say: "Fly under the radar" or "Don't make yourself a target." Bandits in those days would attack a person and strip them of their clothes and all their money. However, in the Semitic culture, there was a sort of *honor* among bandits and if they found you had no money or no extra clothes they would leave you alone and sometimes they would even share with you what money or goods they had. Basically Jesus was telling his disciples to remain poor or poverty stricken, then you have nothing to lose and bandits will leave you alone.

You might think the Roman soldiers would patrol the trails at day and at night, but that was not the case. Roman soldiers pay was very meager, if they got paid at all. When the government got around to paying their soldiers, their money passed through so many hands that by the time the soldier got his pay—well, if you think you don't have anything left on your pay check after the Federal, State, County and City takes their cut, consider the plight of the poor Roman soldier. As a result of this these night time bandits were often the soldiers themselves moonlighting to make up for their minimum wage day jobs.

So when the disciples *'azal or followed* Jesus, this was no glamorous, vacation type, photo op missionary trip where they traveled protected by local police, air marshals, entrance security and government protection, this was following Jesus into the Lawndale section of Chicago, into the hood and witnessing right in the crack houses.

But soft, when Jesus called Philip to *follow* him in verse 43, he used the word *'etha* which also means to follow, but this is not necessarily a following to death, but a following to produce something, a following where you will not return empty handed. This is a business trip where the company sends you out, pays your plane fare, hotel stay, and meals, with expectations that you will return with a signed contract.

You see when Jesus calls us, He may not necessarily be calling us to *'azal or follow* Him into dangerous situations where we may have to lay down our lives. That may or may not be the case, but one thing is for sure if He calls us, He is calling us to *'etha* follow Him to get results and to be productive.

DAY 19

My Servant (Avadi)

JEREMIAH 25:9: "BEHOLD, I will send and take all the families of the North, saith the LORD, and Nebuchadnezzar the king of Babylon, my servant . . ."

I noticed a spike in my book sales on Amazon, in fact it made it into Amazon's Top 100 Best Sellers List at 14 in the category of Christian Reference and 24 in Christian Bible. Ok, no big thing, there are many categories where books are listed, and this was just for the E-book and you move in and out of the list every day. But there are ten million books on Amazon and over two million on E-Book and the vast majority of these books never get close to a Best Sellers List. So it was enough to signal a real wake up call to me. This, coming on the tail of my preparations for a weekend conference, and looking at the Stats on my website and seeing hits from over 60 countries and I suddenly sat up and asked: "Oh my gosh, what am I doing? I mean people are reading this stuff."

With the recent release of the movie *Anna Karenina* I could not help but think of Tolstoy who was just a writer but somehow started a whole non-violent movement of Christian

Anarchists and Anarchist Pacifism in Russia. Thousands of people began following an ascetic path due to his influence. Tolstoy on the other hand, wondering what all the fuss was about as he was just writing a bunch of personal ideas and ponderings that he himself was not that sure about.

At the age of 40,Tolstoy suffered a moral crisis in his life leading to a genuine personal experience with Jesus. He spent the rest of his life searching to understand the heart of God through a study of the teachings of Jesus and taking a literal interpretation of the Sermon on the Mount. Many of his writings reflected this journey, such as his work *"The Kingdom of God Within You"* which greatly influenced the non-violent teachings of Gandhi and Martin Luther King, Jr.

Tolstoy died at the age of 82 when he decided that there must be something to all the fuss over his study on asceticism and thought he would give it a try for himself. He set out on a solitary journey to follow the path of a wandering ascetic in the middle of winter. This journey lasted only two days when he caught pneumonia and died at the Astapovo train station.

The point is that Tolstoy was so wrapped up in trying to understand his relationship with God that he never realized that God would use his spiritual journey to one day influence some key people to follow a path of non-violence.

In no way, shape or form do I come even near the stature of Tolstoy, but I surly cannot help but understand Tolstoy's amazement over people taking him seriously. My journey to understand God's heart and to learn how to study the Word of God, pray, and worship with my heart and not my mind is a personal journey. My method of study is to write and of course a writer likes to see his works published in some way. The fact that someone actually reads his writings often comes as a great surprise. In learning that people actually read what I am writing, I cannot help but pray: "Uh, God, are you sure we ought to let other people in on my ponderings with you? I mean what if someone really takes me seriously?"

I went to bed last night really agonizing over this issue. Should I really be sharing my personal journey, I mean there are actually people following my journey, what if they take me more seriously than I really take myself?" I woke up this morning repeating over and over Hebrew word *avadi* which means *my servant*. Actually, this title was given to Moses, the Messiah and three times to Nebuchadnezzar. Nebuchadnezzar was a godless, pagan Babylonian king. His name is an Akkadian name built on the word Nebu who was the Babylonian deity of wisdom and the son of the God Marduk who was the Babylonian sun God, a throwback to the ancient Phoenician gun god Koster represented by the Taw in the Canaanite script (wrongly referred to as the Ancient Hebrew script). The Taw in the Canaanite script is an **X** which is often mistaken for a picture of a cross.

Yet, here is a pagan king, with a name honoring a pagan god that God Jehovah calls his *avadi* or my servant. Nebuchadnezzar did not knowingly or intentionally serve God, yet God still used him as an *avadi (servant of God)*. The very nature of the word *avadi* suggest looking beyond the surface, something much deeper than one's natural understanding as pictured in the first letter Ayin. The second letter, the Beth, represents the heart of God and the final letter, the Daleth represents a portal to God's knowledge. The final Yod pictures a messenger being sent from heaven.

In other words, an *avadi* is a servant who serves the heart of God and the Ayin suggest that he may not even be aware of it.

So perhaps in my quest to discover God's heart, I am an *avadi*, I may be serving God's heart without being aware of it. I may never really know, but as long as there is an Internet I will keep posting my ponderings. If anyone reads them, I will let God deal with that. As far as I am concerned, I just want to know His heart and if anyone wants to join me on my journey, they are welcomed, but I strongly suggest you follow your own heart and don't take me too seriously.

Day 20

Beloved of Friend ('Ehevath Re'a)

Hosea 3:1: "Then said the LORD unto me, Go yet, love a woman beloved of *her* friend, yet an adulteress, according to the love of the LORD toward the children of Israel, who look to other gods, and love flagons of wine."

I know I was able to reach out and touch the heart of God during my week of silence for ever since that time I find myself weeping for no reason at all. I have even taken to wearing sunglasses all day so people will not see my red eyes. The word *weep* in Hebrew is *baki* which has a numerical value of 42. The word *heart (lev)* also has a numerical value of 42. Weeping comes from the heart. When I find myself weeping for no apparent reason I am now fully aware it is God's heart that is weeping. This morning I felt God's heart and wept. I saw him holding the heart of someone who will read this study and He was speaking Hosea 3:1 repeating the words *"beloved of friend."*

It is a very curious statement, because Hosea was not commanded to love Gomer in Hosea 1:2? Actually in verse 1:2 he is told to *take* a woman of prostitution's. Now in verse 3:1 he is commanded to *love a woman beloved of her friend.* In those days people did not get married out of love, marriages were arranged, fathers would offer a dowry or money to a man to marry off a daughter and men often married more for money than out of love. The idea that a person would marry a woman out of love was radical, almost scandalous. Yet, it was not unheard of and people did break with the conventions at time and marry out of love. Thus, when it came time for Hosea to find a wife, God said to *take* a woman. The word *take* in Hebrew is *qach* from the root *laqach* which means to *take a wife*, but it is also used for *taking possession of something, or capturing something*. Hosea was not asked to *love* Gomer in 1:2 but simply to marry her. But now in 3:1 after she has prostituted herself, taken on many lovers, Hosea is now commanded to *love* his wife.

Some translations say: "Show your love" or "love again." Yet, that is not what it says in Hebrew text. That is only a translator's paraphrase. Actually, the KJV is really the most literal, "*love a woman.*" Actually, the word for *woman* '*ishah* is the same word used for *wife*. Translators use the English word *woman* because it is generally believed that Hosea divorced his wife and so she was not longer a wife. This is based upon verse 2:2 where Hosea says he is neither Gomer's husband nor is she his wife. Actually, in those days a man could have many wives according to the laws of man, but he really only had one woman that he would call his wife, which was the woman he loved. David had many legal wives, but only one was recognized in God's eyes as his actual wife, that was Bathsheba, it was from her blood line that Jesus was born. She was not David's first wife, who was Micah, but she was the woman that was his beloved, the one he was truly intimate with. In Hosea 2:2 when he says that Gomer is no longer his wife, he was not saying he divorced her, but that he no longer shares the intimacies of his heart with her.

In Shakespeare's play, *Julius Caesar*, Portia is grieved that her husband Brutus will not share the secrets of his heart with her. In Act 2 Scene 1 we have this exchange

Portia: *Is my place only on the outskirts of your happiness? If it's nothing more than that, then I'm your whore, not your wife.*

Burtus: *You are my true and honorable wife, as dear to me as are the ruddy drops that visit my sad heart.*

Portia: *If this is true, then should I know this secret?*

Even in Shakespeare's day the distinction between a lover and a wife was made as a wife is more than just a lover but one who shares the secrets of a man's heart and he share hers. So Hosea is still married to Gomer, but since he does not share the secrets of her heart nor hers with his, he does not recognize the relationship as husband and wife.

Not only is Hosea commanded to *love* Gomer, but it is also declared that he is her one true friend: "Beloved of her friend." The word *beloved* in Hebrew is 'ehevath from the root word *'ahav"* used as a Qal participle. As a participle it would have the idea of a continuing love or everlasting love. More specifically 'ehevath, in this context, represents a love from the very heart of God. The word has the suffix, Taw, at the end and would suggest a love of adoration. The word *friend* is re'a in Hebrew and the Masoretes gave it a curious pointing because it clearly displays a play on two root words *ra'ah* and *ravah*. *Ra'ah* expresses a consuming passion. Hosea not only loved Gomer, he had a consuming passion for her. Yet, there is that subtle play on the word *ravah* which means to be hurt or wounded. Hence, *"beloved of friend"* actually means one you have loved and carried a consuming passion for, yet that individual has deeply hurt and betrayed that love. That is why God commanded Hosea to *love* Gomer in the first part of this verse. Hosea had every reason to hate and despise Gomer for her betray of his love and passion, yet he was to continue to love her.

So it is with God towards us. We have betrayed his love and passion for us. He has every reason to be angry with us, condemn us, punish us, send us to hell for the hurt and pain we brought to His heart, yet He continues to love us and forgive us.

This morning I entered God's heart and watched him weep over a heart that deeply wounded his heart. I saw him weep for one that once loved him dearly but went after other gods and hasn't prayed or sought him for a long time. I did not see an angry God, one who was ready to punish this person, divorce this person, send this person to hell for the betrayal, but only a God who wept with a broken heart and continued to love and long to share his passion once again with that person.

DAY 21

Bring it to Pass (Ya'aseh)

PSALMS 37:5 "COMMIT THY way unto the Lord; trust also in Him and he shall bring it to pass."

Practically every modern translation will translate this verse similar to the KJV. I suspect the reason is that you are playing with a very powerful verse and translators do want to be quite careful in what they translate. After all "he shall bring it to pass" is very definite and this verse contains the conditions by which He shall bring it (desires of your heart v. 4) to pass.

First we need to ask, is it that definite that if we commit our way to the Lord and trust Him, He will bring it to pass?" The word for *bringing it to pass* is *ya'aseh* and means to work, fabricate, create, accomplish, and perform. It is in a qal imperfect form. "Bring it to pass" is correct but it does not carry the punch that most modern translation use and that is "He will do it." There is no way around it, this promise is clearly stating that if we commit our way to God and trust Him he will give us the desires of our heart—point blank.

Now the only question is: "What does it mean to commit your way to the Lord." The word commit is *gol* and actually does not mean *commit* although that is what is implied. You have two possible root words depending on whether you put the dot above the *Vav* or below the *Gimmel*. The root word could be *gayal* which means to spin around in a circle for pure joy or it could be *galal* which means to roll together. It is this rolling together where the translators get the idea of commit. Commit is rolling your way into the way of the Lord. We get the same idea if we use the root *gayal* but this time it is rolling our way into the way of the Lord in rejoicing. It is the picture of making bread which is combining all the ingredients and rolling them together into a mound of dough. Sometimes it is done by spinning the ingredients around.

Ancient Jewish teachings tell us that the *Gimmel* in the word *gol* represents a camel. In fact the *Gimmel* shares the same root as *camel* or *gammal*. The camel can journey long days in the desert without drinking water. It carries within itself an internal source of nourishment and replenishment. The Gimmel in the word *gol* encourages us that even though we are traveling through a long, hot, dry and intimidating desert we have within us the resources to survive. The word *way* is *derek* which means a journey, a treading, traveling. The *Gimmel* in *gol* will suggest that this journey may be long, hot and dry, traveling for long periods without encouragement or replenishment. Yet, if you keep rolling or spinning yourself with God, He will give you the desires of your heart.

What is the journey that we take? It is *derek* (Daleth, Resh, Kap), the doorway to a heart filled with the Spirit and power of God. We learn in verse 4 that if we delight ourselves in the Lord He will give us the desires of our heart. This is sort of a catch 22. If we delight ourselves in the Lord, our desires and His desires are the same. But the following verse lays out the conditions. Obtaining the desires of our heart is a journey, sometimes a very discouraging journey through a hot dry desert. Some Christians really long for a ministry and yet they feel like they are accomplishing nothing. They cry out to God: "When will you open up my ministry, when will you give me the desires of my heart which are you desires as well." Sometimes they are ready to just give up, there appears no end to the long hot desert journey to their ministry. Yet the *Gimmel* tells us we have the resources to continue. Not only continue on the journey but to dance and spin in rejoicing in the Lord while on the journey and if you keep *trusting* in the Lord, it will come to pass. You have crossed the desert and have earned the right to instruct others in crossing their own desert.

The word trust *batach* is very much related to *gol* in that is means to join or combine your way with God's way. Batach has the idea of welding together, and *gol* the idea of combining. Both words tell us that the important thing to our journey to receiving the desire of our hearts is to stay wrapped up in the desires and ways of God.

DAY 22

Chariots (Rakah)

II KINGS 6:17: "AND Elisha prayed, and said, LORD, I pray thee, open his eyes, that he may see. And the LORD opened the eyes of the young man; and he saw: and, behold, the mountain *was* full of horses and chariots of fire round about Elisha."

So I find myself praying the Elisha prayer: "Lord, open my eyes that I may see." If God ever answers that prayer, I wonder if I will see horses of fire and chariots of fire? Even as a child listening to the story of Elisha's servant and his seeing the chariots and horses of fire I felt something disturbing about it. Does God really need an army of foot soldiers to defend us. You read further in this story and you find that God never used his army to do battle with the army of Syria. What God simply did was strike all the soldiers blind. No need for swords, horses, chariots and a bloody battle, just a little *poof* and the army is frozen in its tracks and willing to be led by one little servant of God.

Now stop and consider. If you were faced with an angry mob ready to tear you apart and God gives you a vision of a bunch of fiery horses and chariots standing by, would that give you any comfort. Well not to me because I know of no Scriptural record of these fiery horses and chariots ever entering into battle with an earthly or fleshly foe. Usually God deals with a threatening army by using simple things, for instance making four lepers appear like a massive army and scaring the pants off of battle ready soldiers. In the case of Gideon and Jehoshaphat God caused confusion in the camp of the enemy such that they killed each other off. Even when God uses His heavenly special ops to waste the enemy it is usually just one lone angel or maybe just Himself as in the book of Revelation, not a massive army. Come on, does He really need an army to support Himself against us mortals? It is sort of like the scene in Indiana Jones where he confronts a brawny, martial arts expert welding a massive sword. It looks like our hero is dead meat but all he does is calmly pull out a modern day revolver and years of martial arts training and a sharp sword in the hands of one trained in how to use it is instantly dropped.

I mean when a crisis erupts in the Middle East, the United States sends in its Seventh Fleet as a display of power to flex its muscle and the crisis seems to cool down without a shot being fired. Is that what God is doing in II Kings 6:17? Maybe, except the Syrian army never sees the chariots of fire and, in fact, throughout the entire narrative, they are not even aware of their existence to be terrorized by it. Why show the army to the servant? Show it to the Syrians and let them scramble in terror. But then again, maybe they did see something.

Perhaps they saw something so powerful it blinded them as it did Paul on the Damascus Road. Let's just think out of the box for a moment and consider a possible alternative to the renderings of Hebrew words *rakah (chariots) and sus (horses)*. What other renderings of *rakah* are there other than chariots and for *sus* other than horses that could be a picture of what Elisha's servant saw that would bring him comfort, and what the Syrian army saw that would strike them blind and cause them to calmly and humbly submit to the direction of God's prophet?

I certainly do not want to disrupt all those Sunday School teachers who for centuries have taught that Elisha's servant actually saw chariots and horses on fire. I just want to stress that there are alternatives to many of the ancient Hebrew words that we just take for granted as meaning just one thing.

Looking at the word for *chariot* we find that its original use was to express a mode of transportation. Since a chariot was the common mode of transportation for an ancient army we have attached the English word *chariot* to rakah. Actually a rakah could be a tank, jet aircraft, or even a warship. It might be a starship, or a go kart. In other words a *rakah* is simply a mode of transportation. Tracing the word *rakah* through the Akkadian language I found it used to represent a mode of transportation through portal between the earth and heaven. The word for *horse* is *sus* which really means a force or power which moves you from this one point to another. In ancient times that was often a horse which is why *sus* took on the meaning of a horse. Today we have developed other means of moving ourselves from one point to another by a motorized engine. Yet, we too, doggedly cling to the word *horse* when we say that our car engine has so much horse power. In its rawest form *sus* means a power which can move you from one spot to another.

You know I have heard and read many stories of people who claim to have visited heaven. The only stories I truly believe are the ones told by people who express the words of Paul. "I have seen things too wonderful to describe." The only way to describe the supernatural is to put it in terms of the natural. If someone says they saw an actually chariot pulled by horses in heaven, I am hanging on to my wallet. But if that person says: "The only way I can describe it is like a chariot pulled by horses, but that is not what I really saw." I will ease up a little.

So what did Elisha's servant see? I have no idea as he saw into the supernatural world and only those given a glimpse of the supernatural and God's glory can understand it. Elisha prayed that God would *open the eyes* of his servant. The word *open* is *pakah* in Hebrew, it is the word that is used for the opening of a door from a prison or confined spaced to view and enter the outside world. It is the same word used in the Akkadian language for the *opening of a portal* to the dwelling place of the gods.

I can only say this in my opinion. Elisha had a pure heart and hence he was continually seeing an open portal to heaven, this is the same portal that he saw his mentor Elijah pass through. We render this as chariots of fire and its horses, but what he saw was too wonderful to describe. They were on fire, which is really the only natural way to express the loving (fiery) passion of God. He prayed that his servant could view this loving passion of God and having lived with a man of God and having a heart open to God he was allowed to see this open portal into the loving passion of God for the sake of Elisha and it brought him comfort. The Syrian army did not have a heart for God; all they saw was a bright light which blinded them so they could not see this loving passion of God.

Then again as I pray for God to open my eyes, I find myself praying that my eyes will be *pakah (opened)*. Perhaps my study here is nothing more than wishful thinking that I will catch a glimpse of this loving passion of God. In my three score years on this natural earth I am beginning to realize that the heart can see things that the physical eye will never see. So I will follow the example of John the Baptist, Paul and even Jesus Himself and spend time in desert solitude where I will pray that I can begin to see and hear with my heart and not with my physical eyes and ears.

DAY 23

Whom I Desired (Chimadeti)

SONG OF SOLOMON 2:3: "As the apple tree among the trees of the wood, so is my beloved among the sons. I sat down under his shadow with great delight, and his fruit was sweet to my taste."

As I was reading this passage in my Hebrew Bible I was struck by the word *chimadeti (great delight)*. That word was strangely out of place in this sweet romantic verse. I was intrigued as to how our English translators had handled this word. I first went to your friend and mine, the King James Version which rendered it as "great delight." This seemed to be the good cowardly way out. Other modern translations said the same. Some simply rendered it as "delight." One translation was a little braver and said "with *whom I desired*". But the version with the most guts rendered this word as *have I raptured.*

What caught my attention in the use of the word *chimadeti* is that it is used only once in the Song of Solomon and its rooted in the same word that is used in Exodus 20:17: *"Thou shalt not covet."* If you ever go to a synagogue and glance at the Ten Commandments above the ark and scroll down to the 10th commandment you will see in Hebrew Script the words "Lo tachmod" (lit. no you will covet). Yet, in the same synagogue I saw a Jewish woman pick up her granddaughter, kiss her and say: "Come chamudi." I took a look at the 10 commandment and asked my host: "What did she just call the child?" My host explained it was modern Hebrew for "my precious one." I followed by asking: "Is that not rooted in the same word in the tenth commandment for *covet?*" He merely shrugged as if to say: "Go figure." How Hebrew managed to meander around the guilt inducing "thou shalt not covet" to the Modern Hebrew "my precious one" proved to be an irresistible study.

First I realized that the commandment was not a blanket "you will not covet" but "you will not covet anything that belongs to your neighbor." We interpret this word *chamed* or *covet* as *having a desire for something that does not belong to us.* That idea has always been troubling to me because I can barely walk out of the door in the morning before I start desiring things that I do not have. The command is specific; you do not desire what is intimate or being consumed by your neighbor. Just a simple desire cannot hurt. *Chamed* has to carry a little more punch than that. I had an e-mail this morning from someone asking about the "Garden of Eden." I was drawn to the passage in Genesis 2:9 "And out of the ground made the Lord God to grow every tree that is pleasant to the sight." There it is again, *chamed,* only it is translated by practically every translation as *pleasant or nice to look at.* Only one modern translation used the word *desirable.* Of course, we learn later just how seductive that can be.

Early rabbinic literature showed a sexual connotation to *chamed* as *chamdam,* using it as a reference to a *lustful person. Chimmud* is even blunter as a reference to a sexual appetite. As a verb *chamed* means to be *excited or hot.* Hebrew Jewish grammarian David Kimhi (Radak) states that it is no coincidence that the word *cham* (hot), makes up two thirds of the root. He points out that *lechem chamudot* is taken by some to mean *fresh, hot tasty bread.*

So what I am drawing from this? Is Solomon's beloved saying she is sitting under the apple tree with one hot number? Well, there is much more to my research on this verse that I cannot put into a short study, so I am leaving open a number of gaps, but let me just share my conclusion on Song of Solomon 2:3. The young lover is making a very distinct play on the word *chamed* by bringing it into association with the *apple tree* among the trees of the woods. This is a direct reference to the *forbidden fruit* of the Garden of Eden. She sits under her beloved's shadow with *covertness* or *chamed* eating this forbidden fruit. You see the word *chamed* ultimately has the idea of intimacy or totally possessing and consuming something. This fruit is not forbidden so long as she consumes it within the bounds of intimacy born out of love with her beloved. Just as a sexual relationship is forbidden outside marriage born out of love so was the forbidden fruit in the garden forbidden outside the intimacy and love with relationship with God.

You see, Adam and Eve were permitted to possess everything in the Garden of Eden except the fruit of one tree. Oral tradition teaches that this forbidden fruit wasn't off limits to man, but only to Adam or Eve without the intimate presence and love with a relationship with God. This fruit was designed by God to be the *bedroom* so to speak with God and shared personally between two people, God and His beloved. Just as a husband and wife will share the fruits of their intimacy in a bedroom totally alone with no one around watching or listening, so God created this *tree* with its *fruits* to be shared with Himself and Adam alone or Eve alone. Sin did not occur until Eve shared the fruit with Adam, then she was sharing the one thing she was not allowed to share with her husband, that *fruit* that was meant for her and God alone. The penalty for Eve and her female descendants was that her "desire will be for her husband but he will rule over her. (Genesis 3:16)." This is another study in Hebrew but basically what it means is that a woman will try to gain from her husband that special love that only God can give. If she turns to her husband for it she will become frustrated and perhaps angry with her husband because He will be unable to give her what she deeply desires, something only God can give. Her husband will "rule over her" or he will become frustrated because he cannot provide this special intimacy with her. Only God can fill this gap in the relationship.

He is still a personal God and although He allows us to share everything about our relationship with Him with others in the deepest *koinonia (communion by intimate participation)*; there is still a special intimacy that He has reserved for us and us alone where our love for Him and His for us is consummated. No one can share in the *fruit* of that for that belongs to God and no one else. He is, after all, a *jealous God*, who longs for a special, intimate time with each one of us that is shared with no one else, just as a husband

and wife share an intimacy with each other that no one else in the world will share. We enter into this intimacy with God through the blood of Jesus Christ and it is through His blood that we can eat of this forbidden fruit because only through the complete cleansing of the blood of Jesus are we worthy to partake in this most intimate fruit to be shared with God alone and no one else.

There is a Biblical expression that I found also uses the word "chamed" which is appropriate to end this study; "Va-yelekh belo chemdah" I will take my leave without anyone regretting my departure.

Day 24

Prayer (Tepel or Palal)

PSALMS 65:2: "O THOU that hears prayer, unto thee all flesh shall come."

It is amazing that the word for *hears* is *shama*. The normal rendering for *shama* is *to hear* but as we find in Isaiah 1;19 it is also rendered as *obedience*. This is really the basic intent of the word *shama*. Of course we are not going to render that word in Psalm 65:2 as *obey*. I mean we certainly do not want to give the impression that God is at our beck and call which is what our English understanding of the word *obey* conveys to us. This word *shama* is very difficult to translate as we really do not have an English word to convey its intent. If we render it as *hear* that is not really expressing its true nature as that conveys the idea that God is listening but does not necessary act on what he *hears*. To render the word *obey* is not accurate in the sense that it gives the idea of being in some way subservient. The word *shama* finds itself somewhere in the middle. Give me a word for a loving mother preparing for her child's birthday party. The child is all excited about getting a birthday cake, ice cream and a new video game. The child never questions that he will get a birthday party. To him the positive response to his request for a birthday party is just a given, he would be absolutely surprised if he did not get one. The only thing is that when the birthday party comes, instead of getting a birthday cake and ice cream he gets carrot sticks and celery and when he opens his present in front of all his friends he finds it is not the latest version of the video game Man Slaughter, but a new pair of underwear. Give me a word for that expression of love and you have a good word for *shama* which can be used in this verse.

There seems to be a remez here. Why would the passage not say: "You who hear prayers all flesh will come to you *in prayer*." All flesh will come to God but not all flesh will pray to God. If we take a closer look at this word used here for prayer you will see something very interesting. The root word for prayer is *palal*, which has the idea of interceding and supplication, i.e., to earnestly and humbly plead or beg.

This gets complicated when we find that the word *basar* (flesh) is used rather than *adam* or *ish* which is the more common word for *man*. *Basar* speaks of the inner part of natural man. This is not the soul but one's natural inner desires. It doesn't take any stretch of the imagination that all people (all flesh) at some time or another in their lives comes to God with petitions. Everyone gets themselves into some sort of bind where they inwardly call out to God with a petition. And this passage says that God hears and acts on all these petitions. It seems to be quite obvious that God does not act upon all petitions. Yet, in truth, this verse is saying that He does act on all petitions.

This is why we see that there is a difference in *prayer* and in *coming* to God. A lot of people *come* to God but not everyone *prays* to God. You see the word *prayer* (Heb. *palal*) is found in a rather unusual form here. In this verse the form it takes is *tepilah*. Now *tepilah* could come from one of two different roots. It could come from the root word *palal* or it could also take the root word *tapel*. Actually, with this being Hebrew poetry, it is mostly like a play of the two words. It is intentionally placed in this particular form to express both root words. Where *palal* has the idea of a sincere, humble petition and supplication to God, *tapel* carries the idea of unseasoned, unsavory, foolish or impiety. When we come to God we can come to Him in one of two ways. We can come as *palal (sincere, humble petition)* or as *tapel (foolishly)*. Yet, God will still hear and act.

The difference is that if we are coming to God as *tapel* with a request for a birthday party with cake, ice cream and the latest video game (things that He may deem as harmful to us), God will still hear and act on our prayer except He answers by giving us something that is beneficial and practical to us such as carrot sticks, celery and underwear (which could be embarrassing). He has acted upon our request, but since it is so far removed from what we asked for we don't even recognize it as God responding to our request.

When we come to God with our petitions are we coming to Him in *palal* humility and supplication or *tepel* foolishness and impiety? Either way He will act on our request, but if we come to him in *tepel (foolishness and impiety)* we may never even recognize that God is responding. The important thing to keep in mind is that God does hear and respond when we come to him. It is just that most of the time we come to him in *tepel (foolishness and impiety)* and not *palal* (sincere and humbly) and hence we don't even recognize the response.

DAY 25

The Fourth Generation (Rova')

NUMBERS 23:10: "WHO CAN count the dust of Jacob and the number of the fourth part of Israel?"

Balak is trying to get Balaam to curse Israel and instead he ends up blessing Israel. It has not quite dawned on Balak that God is not at man's beck and call. He figured if Balaam was a prophet he would have some pull with God and if he paid Balaam well enough he could finagle God to put a curse on Israel. I know that sounds ridiculous. It is about as ridiculous as asking a pastor or priest to pray for you because he should be able to persuade God to answer your prayer simply because he is a minister. Just because someone seems to be more holy than you or has some special office does not mean he or she has God at their beck and call. You have just as much clout with God as Billy Graham. Balaam knew he had no special pull with God; even though he was a prophet. That is why he said: "Who can count the dust of Jacob and the number of the fourth part of Israel? The *fourth part* in Hebrew is simply *rova'* which is the word for *four*.

Practically every translation renders this the same as the KJV. They assume Balaam is making a reference to the number and might of Israel. One commentator even says that when he refers to the *fourth part*, it is a reference to the four divisions of Israel (Jamison Brown commentary). He was referring to the military strength of Israel.

This does not make much sense. It would seem that Balaam is telling Balak that he cannot curse Israel because of their great numbers. He just got done asking: "How can I curse that which God has not cursed?" Their numbers have nothing to do with whether or not Balaam can curse Israel.

When I started to research this in Jewish literature I found something quite amazing. First, the use of the words Jacob and Israel for the nation of God is a reference to the generations of Israel. Jacob represents the female aspect of the nation and Israel represents the male aspect. The two who join together to conceive a child. The word *dust* is *'apar* which is also used for a young man. The numerical value of *'apar* is 350 which is the same numerical value for a young woman. Hence the sages consider Balaam's reference as reference to the generations. But that is moving into a deeper understanding. In the literal understanding they view the term dust as a reference to humility and prayer to God. The sons of Jacob were people who had humbled themselves and prayed before God. Balaam is looking to the up and coming generation, the generation that would have the faith to enter the Promised Land. More than that, this is the fourth generation of Israel. There were four generations of Israel represented, each generation representing 40 years. Balaam was counting from the birth of Moses. The first generation of Israel was when Moses grew up in Pharaoh's court. The second generation was when Moses was in exile, the third generation when Moses lead the people out of Egypt and now the fourth generation who were growing up to be the ones who would enter the promised land. There is a belief that the fourth generation would be the mightiest in the power and knowledge of God because they would have the strongest faith. So Balaam was saying: "How can I curse a people who are not only a people who humble themselves in prayer to God, but represent the fourth and most powerful generation?"

I remember watching a presentation on PBS, Nova about the Monarch butterfly. Every year the fourth generation of the Monarch butterfly will take a three month journey. They will fly 50 miles a day from Canada to one spot down in Mexico. They will fly from all parts of Canada and converge in Texas and fly into Mexico arriving almost at the same time. There are millions of them who all arrive on this one mountain in Mexico. What caught my attention was that this is the fourth generation that makes this 3,500 mile trip. The documentary showed how many suffered and died to make this journey. Some died from the weather, the elements, or predators. In fact they are on that journey right now to their promised land and they should be passing through the Chicago area about this time.

Is this a sign or a reminder from God? What is the nature of this reminder? The sages teach that not only is there something special with each fourth generation, but that there are four generations in our relationship with God. The first is your spiritual birth, I would say your rebirth in Jesus, the second is your growing period, the third is your wilderness generation and the fourth is your entrance into the Promised Land. If you feel you've been wandering in the wilderness like Israel was at the time of Balaam, and you feel like you are getting nowhere and accomplishing nothing, like Israel must have felt, then you need to look up and see the Monarchs flying to Mexico for they are reminding you that you are in that fourth generation and the Promise Land is sight. You may have a few more storms and a few more predators, but if you can continue your journey, you will arrive on the mountain top where, like the Monarchs, you can rest from your long journey.

As Israel wandered in the wilderness, they must have felt abandoned by God, or felt pretty hopeless. Yet Balaam saw what they did not see. He saw a praying people who were in the fourth generation and he was not about to curse a praying people, let alone one that was into their fourth generation.

DAY 26

When I am Afraid (Yom 'Ira')

PSALMS 56:3 "WHAT TIME I am afraid, I will trust in thee. In God I will praise His Word, in God I will put my trust; I will not fear what flesh can do unto me."

Verse 3 gives a rather strange combination of words. "What time I am afraid" does sound awkward, but it is very close to the original Hebrew. The expression is "yom 'ira'." It could be rendered literally as "a day that I am fearing." All of us have some day off in the future that we dread. It may be a coming exam, a yearly review at your job, tax time, or maybe even the coming holiday season. Since it is a future event, we tend to put it out of our minds until some little occurrence jogs our memory and instantly that sense of dread comes back. Or we may be like Charlie Brown who walks around with a storm cloud over his head and his head alone. We are just in constant stress over some future event.

The grammatical structure of verse 3 is a little odd for the context. David is reflecting on his capture by the Philistines at Gath and then he says: "The day that I am fearing . . ." The event is over with, so what does he fear?

There was a time when Abraham Lincoln was the President that his wife got herself in some financial problem which could have been a real scandal for the presidency. Secretary Seward managed to deflect the scandal and resolve the issue. Secretary Seward went to President Lincoln and reported that the scandal involving his wife was now resolved and closed. President Lincoln showed no joy but only became very melancholy and went to his desk, sat down and hung his head. Secretary Seward spoke up: "Mr. President, perhaps you misunderstood, the problem with your wife is resolved." President Lincoln quietly replied: "I know it's resolved, I'm just getting ready to worry about the next problem she will cause." "What problem is that," inquired Seward." President Lincoln replied: "I don't know but there will be one."

This is most likely the case with David. The problem with the Philistines had long been resolved, but David knew that his future held many similar problems. Reflecting on his experience with the Philistines probably jogged his memory that he had another stressful situation facing him in the future but his response was: "I will trust in thee." I fully expected to find the word *batach* for trust to be in a participial form. It is not, it is in a simple qal future form. David is confronting a future problem and he is saying: "I will trust in the Lord." This is not David's style of writing. To be typical of David's style he would have made this a participle putting this in a present tense: "I am trusting in the Lord."

As I meditated on this, I realize that this is typical David. In Matthew 6:34 Jesus instructed us to not worry about tomorrow for tomorrow will take care of itself. Each day has enough trouble of its own. David was simply following this advice. There was no sense in trusting God for something that hasn't yet appeared on the horizon. David could have said: "God I am trusting you for the day the Assyrians show up at my door. I am trusting you to take care of me; I am trusting you for favor." Yet, he would just be worrying and fretting about the event rather than simply saying: "Hey, if that happens, I will simply trust God at that time the way I did when I was taken captive with the Philistines." David refused to walk around with that storm cloud over his head. I don't know about you but I tend to find myself in the President Lincoln mode rather than the David mode saying: "Well that problem is resolved, not what am I going to do when the next problem shows up?" The fact is I am going to do with the next problem what I did with the last problem. I am going to trust God and I am going to watch Him deliver me like he did with the last problem.

In Psalm 56:3 David is declaring that he was not going to live from problem to problem, rather he was going to put all future problems in the hands of the God that he loved and just live from glory to glory. If the problem arises at some future day, he will simply say: "God, this is that problem I told you about a couple months ago, I put it in your hands— remember? Well I am now going to just trust in you." That word *trust (betach)* is a word I have mentioned in a past study. It means to cling to, adhere to or in a modern sense, to be welded to. David is also saying that he was melted into God. His problems were God's problem.

Calvin Coolidge was once asked by a reporter why he appeared so calm when he was burdened with the office of the President. He replied: "If I see ten problems walking down the road, I know that nine will fall into a ditch before they ever reach me."

So the next time you find yourself worrying over some future problem that hasn't even come down the road yet, just do what David did. Pray and say: "Well, Lord, if that problem ever reaches me it is our problem. It is your problem just as well as mine, and I don't know what to do. But when and if the day of the problem arises, I am just going to trust you to do something, like you did in the past when I faced similar problems. In the meantime I will just deal with today."

Day 27

Angel Food (Lechem 'Abirim)

PSALMS 78:25: "MAN DID eat angels' food: he sent them food to the full."

The Psalmist is retelling the story of the Exodus and God's loving protection over his people. Rather than say he gave them *manna* from heaven he calls it *angel's food*. Today we have what is known as *angel food cake*, so named because it is light and fluffy. The term *angel food cake* was introduced just after the Civil War by a former slave who published a cook book. In this book she had a receipt for, what she called, *angel food cake*. She indicated that friends and relatives would often eat *angel food cake* after a funeral as a reminder that God had sent his angels to take their loved ones home. Perhaps this former slave was closer to the mind of God than many of our translators, theologians, Biblical historians and lexicographers.

As is typical with Semitic storytelling, the storyteller will often interchange a name with a descriptive word. For instance, in the story of Ruth, Elimelech named his two sons Mahlon which means *sickness* and Chilion which means *wasting away*. It stands to reason a Semitic father would never give his sons such names, particularly when there was such a strong belief in that day that a name, when spoken, actually held the power to transform that person into what that name really means. For instance, if a man's named his child Ozaz (*powerful*) then calling that child by that name throughout his life will cause him to become powerful. Considering the fact that Elimelech was a very loving, caring husband and father he would never have cursed his babies with such a name. Yet the storyteller would apply such a name so that the listener would have a better understanding of the story that these two young men were suffering from some health problems.

Considering the nature of Hebrew and Semitic story telling it would not be unreasonable and not a threat to our understanding of the inspiration and infallibility of Scripture to read this term *angel food* as a story telling device, something that God is using to send us a very powerful message. The fact that he inspired the Psalmist to call this *angel food* rather than manna is what the sages would refer to as a remez or a hint of a deeper meaning.

To explore this deeper meaning we need to examine this term *angel food* in the original Hebrew. The term in Hebrew is *lechem 'abirim* which many translators render as *bread of the mighty ones or princes*. The word that is commonly used for *angels* is *male'ale* which means *messengers*. The word rendered as *angels* here, however, is *'abirim* which means *brave, noble, or strong*. This is where the commentators get the idea that this was bread which was eaten only by nobility, kings and princes. They may be right and David was telling them that God gave them the best, most delicious food imaginable and yet the people grew tired of it and demanded some variety and began to complain.

The Talmud teaches that this manna was something else. It was the perfect food, food that was completely absorbed by the body so that there was no waste. The body used this food entirely such that there was no need for the people to eliminate the waste from their bodies. Had their bodies produced waste this would have produced a very real sanitary problem when you have a million or so refugees camping out together. God eliminated this problem by giving them food that was *'abirim*. You see, another meaning of *'abirim* is feathers or something that is as light as feathers. This manna drifted from heaven like a feather drifting off a bird onto the ground and the picture is that this was something from God himself that drifted to earth. Actually, the sages take this further. If we ignore the Masoretic text we find *'abirim* to be a compound word which would mean *the Father who overcomes*. Like a feather off a bird, a feather which causes a bird to fly to the heavens, God shares His *feather* with his loved ones so that they too can and overcome the penalty of their sins and fly to heaven to be with Him. When Jesus said "this is my body, do eat of it" the disciples may very well have thought of the manna and how it was a part of God Himself that would allow them to overcome their sins and one day *fly to heaven*. Perhaps the old slave was right to name the cake that was eaten at funerals *angel food cake* for the departed soul was truly eating of the manna of heaven, taking on that part of God, His Son Jesus, who through his death on the cross provided the *transportation* to heaven.

I believe the Psalmist, under the inspiration of God, choose the words *lechem 'abirim (angels food)* to give a Messianic picture of His Son who would one day come and as the manna gave physical life to the people of Israel, the *lechem 'abirim* would bring spiritual life to those who would trust and believe in Him.

Sometimes I get tired of just eating *angel's food* and start demanding that God do something different with my life, give me a new type of ministry or something more exciting. Yet, every time I eat of the *angel's food* I am reminded that what I have is the best that God has to offer me, sharing *His feathers* or sharing in His presence through the death and resurrection of His Son. Perhaps God whispers to me what he spoke to Israel: "You want more? I have given you My best and that is not good enough?"

Next week I go down South to the State of the Union *where angel food cake* was born and where I will spend a week in silence, feasting on the Manna from heaven or the *lechem 'abirim (angel food)*.

DAY 28

Hedge (Succoth)

JOB 1:9-10: "THEN SATAN answered the Lord and said: Doth Job fear God for naught? Hast thou made an hedge about him, and about his house and about all that he hath on every side? Thou hast blest the work of his hands and his substance is increased in the land."

Hedge—Hebrew: *Succoth*—covering, protection, conceal.

The form used here for the word *hedge* is very unusual. It is found here as *sakath*. This is spelled Shin, Kap and Taw. This particular form could be found in two possible root words which mean almost the same thing except one begins with a Shin and the other begins with a Samek.

Translators go with the root word *sakak* which is spelled Samek, Kap, Kap. This is where we get the word Succoth as in the Feast of Tabernacles. This word means a covering of protection. It is also a word used for weaving or intermingling. God had so intermingled and woven His protection into Job that the enemy could not touch Him without touching God and, of course, the enemy was not about to try and harm God. Once more to even threaten Job would be to threaten God and that would not be a good move on his part.

To get to Job, the enemy had to cause God to *unmingle* Himself from Job. There were only two ways the enemy could get God to *unmingle* Himself from Job. He could get Job to sin and to steer his focus away from God so God would not be able to keep himself mingled or woven into Job. By getting Job to focus on things other than God such as worldly and fleshing concerns old Job would fall out of harmony with God and this wonderful tapestry that God had woven with Job would become completely unraveled. Apparently, the enemy tried that and it didn't work, old Job kept offering sacrifices, kept turning back to God and committing everything back to Him. Every time the enemy attacked Job, Job kept *hitting the mark*. The enemy could not get Job to *miss the mark* (sin—Heb. *chatah*). The only other way was to get God to voluntarily unmingle Himself, to voluntarily lift the *Succoth*.

I believe that is why we have this particular form of the word which suggests a play on the two root words. The other possible root word is *savak* which also means a covering, intermingling or weaving, but this is not a covering or weaving of protection, it is a covering and weaving of the passionate love of God. God could not remove that, He could not unmingle Himself from His passionate love for Job any more than a mother could remove her love for her child. A mother can remove her *sakak* or her arms of protection around her child albeit reluctantly and unwillingly, but it is possible. Yet she cannot willingly remove her *savak*, her love for the child, she cannot stop loving her child. Her child will grow up, maybe join the military and go off to war. She may long to keep her arms around him and protect him, but she must let him go, she can let go of her *sakak*, but she cannot let go of her *savak* her love for the child.

The enemy knew this, but he felt that if God let go of his *sakak* and let him attack all that Job loved on earth, his family, his possessions and reputation, then Job would voluntarily unmingle Himself from God's *savak* or love and he would reject God's love.

God knew Job's heart for Job's heart was joined with God's heart and as a result the enemy could not know Job's heart, he could only guess and he guessed wrong. When God let go of His *sakak*, his protection, his *savak*, his passionate love stayed with Job. When the enemy attacked Job he caught a glimpse of his heart and the enemy knew he was defeated. Job's heart was so intermingled with God's heart, the *savak* was so strong that the enemy could only tuck his tail behind him and wander off in disgrace.

The enemy is still trying to get God to remove his *sakak*, his protection. Old Job was not the first or last one that the enemy used to challenge God to back off from His *sakak* (protection). He may have challenged God to back off from his *sakak*, to get to you. If you find yourself in that situation, remember, God can never back off from His *savak*, his passionate love for you and like Job, you will always have his *savak*, His passionate love no matter how much God allows the enemy to touch you. The rock Job was anchored to (God's passionate love) held, no matter what storms God allowed the enemy to bring. We have that same promise in I Corinthians 10:13 that He will not allow us to be tempted more than we are able to bear and with that temptation, He will provide a way out so you can stand up under it.

DAY 29

Soft Answer (Rakak)

PROVERBS 15:1: "A soft answer turneth away wrath: but grievous words stir up anger"

"But soft, what light on yonder window breaks, it is the East and Juliet is the sun." Shakespeare, *Romeo and Juliet Act 2, Scene 2*

Those who have read my little studies in the past are familiar with a little expression I use: "but soft." Basically, I am just showing off my love of Shakespeare and the old English by using this expression, but, I also use it because there is really no modern term which expresses what the old English can express in this word *soft*.

Most modern translations render Hebrew word *rak* as *gentle*. Ok, *gentle* is a proper rendering of this word but in its context I do not believe it is the right word to use here. Then again neither is the word *soft*. In the day of King James *soft* was an appropriate word to use, but over the last couple hundred years it has lost its meaning. Today when we read this passage as *soft* we automatically think that a quiet, soothing answer will turn away wrath. Sort of like Will Rodgers said: "Diplomacy is the art of saying nice doggy while looking for a big stick." That might work on Sparky, my neighbor's pit bull, but not always on human beings. I learned that much when I worked with troubled teens. Sometimes a quiet answer enraged them all the more as they felt they were being patronized. They felt like they were being treated like some savage wild beast and although they were acting like it, they still did not want to be seen as a savage wild beast.

When Shakespeare used the word *soft* in the context of Romeo seeking Juliet we find that at one moment Romeo is feeling frustrated and then suddenly all that frustration turns to passion as he notices a light in his beloved's window. The very thought of her floods him with passion and love and these feelings serve to soften his troubled heart.

The King James translators choose the word *soft* for Hebrew word *rak* because they understood that the word *rak* comes from the root word *rakak* which means to be *tender or delicate of heart*. It is the expression you use when you see a wounded puppy, or a child struggling or weeping. It is what we feel when we see the devastation after a tornado and see the suffering it left behind. We say: "our hearts go out to them." In old English we would say: "But soft." In other words it is an answer that is filled with the love and compassion that God feels.

This verse is not saying that when someone is expressing anger toward us that if we speak quietly it will cool them down. In some cases it may, in many cases it will not. What it is saying is that when that other driver cuts us off and gives us the three finger salute, we do not return the gesture by shaking our fist. We return the favor with compassion and love. We consider why that person is behaving the way he does and if it is our fault we apologize. If it is not our fault we pray for that person for whatever it is that is causing this dysfunctional behavior. In other words we do what Jesus taught in Matthew 5:44: "Love your enemies, bless them that curse you, do good to them that hate you, pray for them that despitefully use you."

In the Northern dialect of Aramaic Jesus used the word *tob* which we render as *good*. *Tob* is identical to Hebrew word *tov* which means to be in harmony with God. In other words let your response to the one who hates you be in harmony with God's response. God's response is one of love.

I have am beginning to understand what it means to find rest in God's heart. Yesterday, I drove by an abortion clinic where Right to Life protesters stood outside with their signs and banners. One banner had a picture of the horribly mutilated body of a fetus near full term. I guess I watched too many creature features as a kid and saw too many slash movies to be moved by this picture. I saw it and drove on. But suddenly I felt my heart grieving and I was weeping. I instantly knew this was not my grief or my tears. I am never really moved by such pictures, I am too sanitized by Hollywood's B-movies. I never gave much thought about the abortion issue; I had other concerns in my life. Yet, I was moved to tears. I knew and understood that these tears could only be God's tears. In my journey to God's heart, I have to feel God's heart to feel what God feels.

I realized at that moment that God had given me a special gift as a result of my search for His heart, He has allowed my heart to feel the pain in His heart, He has allowed my heart to see these pictures as His heart sees them and He has allowed my heart to hear the voices of the protesters as He hears them. Try as I might, I cannot help but weep as God weeps. I Corinthians 13:13: So now faith, hope, and love abide, these three; but the greatest of these is love (God's love)." To know and experience God's love, to understand what that love is all about has freed me from so many fears for I know that I can rest in that love.

Rak (Soft) expresses the very heart of God. When we respond to wrath with the loving heart of God, that wrath will be turned away, for no one can resist the love of God. Sharing the love of God is not something we work at, struggle to produce, it is the natural result and gift of giving our hearts to God and letting Him share His heart with us. We Christians can be very good at giving our hearts to God, but do we really accept His heart in return? Do we dare to feel what His heart feels, see what His heart sees and hear what His heart hears?

DAY 30

Shield (Magen)

PSALMS 3:3 "BUT THOU O'Lord art a shield to me, the glory and the lifter of my heard."

This Psalm was written in probably the worst moment of David's life. His beloved son, whom David named Absalom which means *father of peace,* had been anything but peaceful. He revolted against his father, started a revolution, seized the throne from his father and sent his father off into exile with a few of his followers and then formed a posse to go out after him and kill him. Then, as if things were not bad enough, as David was fleeing the kingdom with his few loyal followers, some Benjamite starts throwing rocks at him shouting out that he is getting what he deserves.

One of David's loyal servants steps up and says: "Why should this dead dog insult the king, you just say the word and I'll go lop his head off." I have always been moved by David's response. "No, let him throw rocks, perhaps God will have some mercy on me." Here David was at his lowest point, he was a failure as a king, his vocation or career was gone. He had lost everything, his wealth, power, friends, and probably his worst feeling was that he had failed as a father. But I think there was something worse than that; he probably felt he had failed God. I believe when he instructed his servant to let the Benjamite continue throwing rocks at him it was because he really believed God was behind it, that God was trying to show him how he had abused the power He had given him.

I think many of us at one time or another have faced a real failure and as a result of that failure someone starts to throw *rocks* at us. I remember such a time in my life and someone that I had really hurt due to my own selfishness started to throw verbal rocks at me. A loyal friend suggested I not stand for it. But, like David, the only thing I could think was: "No, let that person continue to throw the verbal rocks, perhaps this realization of my personal failure will lead me back to God."

It is at this point that David said the Lord was his shield. The word shield is *magen* which is a play on the word *negan*. *Magen* means a shield and a protector. Indeed the Lord is a shield and protector. The word itself tells you how he becomes a shield. The word is spelled Mem which shows that he protects us through his revealed knowledge which is his Word. The next letter Gimmel tells us that this comes through his loving kindness and the final letter Nun reveals that we must receive this protection through faith. As I said, this is a play on the word *negan* which means music or music played on a stringed instrument. David was a musician who played a stringed instrument. When he would go through a time of stress, he would retreat and play his stringed instrument and in that music he would find a sense of peace. David was not only saying God was his protector, but that God was his source of peace in times of great trial.

Not only that but God was the *lifter* of his head. The word *lifter* is *merim*. This is found in a Hiphil participial form. God is the one who is causing his head to be lifted up. He is totally discouraged. There may have been encouraging reports that all is not lost. He may have had followers who declare their loyalty to him and would fight to the death to reestablish him on his throne. Yet, none of that would encourage him. It was only God and God alone who could encourage him. When things get tough, we look to the natural to encourage us. We see an improvement in the economy, or get a compliment from the boss and suddenly we are encouraged again and our head is lifted up again. Yet, David said that it is God and only God who can lift his head and offer encouragement.

Also this is in a participial form. This would create a picture of God continually lifting David's head. It is almost like God is saying to David, "Come on David, I know you blew it, but look at me." God continually raises David head so he can look at Him and see that He is forgiven, that God still does love him.

When I face my greatest fear, I search through the natural for encouraging signs. Yet the only true source of encouragement lies in the *magen (shield)*, the revealed knowledge of God and his lovingkindness, but it takes the *Nun* faith in that revealed knowledge and loving kindness for it to be a shield.

DAY 31

Everlasting Love ('Al Ken)

JEREMIAH 33:13: "THE LORD hath appeared of old unto me, *saying*, Yea, I have loved thee with an everlasting love: therefore with lovingkindness have I drawn thee."

I have been meditating on the writer's use of the double accusative. He loves us with an everlasting love to draw us to Him. The syntax would suggest that God loves us with an everlasting love so that He can continually draw us to him. I have learned that He is continually drawing us to His heart where we will find true *rest*.

The word for *draw* is *mashak* which is an archer's term for drawing a bow string. When we say an archer is drawing his bow we say he is pulling back on the bow string. The further he pulls back on the bow string, the more the strength or tension of that bow builds until the arrow is released. Drawing the bow spring is a continuing process until the archer feels he has enough strength in his bow to release the arrow. This process of drawing on a bow string has a restraining aspect to it. When drawing the bow you are restraining from releasing the arrow until you have the proper tension on the bow strings, hence the use of the double accusative in this verse.

The word *everlasting is* really two words in a construct form, *'al ken*. It has the idea of *over and above* if we take the most common root word of *'alah*. However, there is another possible root word which is *'alal* and means to roll over or repeat an action. Judging from the syntax of this verse with the use of the double accusative and within its context I would be incline to consider the root word to be *'alal*. Hence, God loves us with a love that is constantly repeating itself. The word *'al* is constructed to *ken*; this might suggest a play on a root word *kanan* which would mean to protect. God is loving us over and over repeatedly to protect us. It is generally agreed, however, that the root word is *kavan* which means to establish, fix or confirm. In other words, *everlasting love* is a love that is a fixed love and just continually repeats itself over and over, it is never ending.

The implications of this are staggering. God's love is so fixed that nothing, absolutely nothing will alter this love. He has established this love to *draw us (mashak)* to Him or to follow a process of strengthening our bond with Him.

However, there is something else that is very apparent in this use of the double accusative. God loves all mankind equally. Lately, the news has been filled with the story of a man who kidnapped three young girls, held them prisoner in his home for ten years and abused them. Does God love such a man as this with an everlasting love? Does He love him just as much as you and I? The answer is "yes" he loves this monster just as much as you or I, but no, He does not love him with an everlasting love. Now let me qualify that with saying I do not know this man's heart, I am only basing my conclusion on his actions and what the news media tells me were his actions. However, based upon that I will make the assumption that even though God does love him he is not returning that love to God, hence God does not love him with an everlasting love. You see, if there was just one accusative in this verse then that would mean everyone qualifies for the everlasting love. But the second accusative *mashak* (draw) limits this love to only those who will receive this love and return it.

With loving kindness *(kasad)* God is drawing us to Himself. There is no high level or lower levels of God's love; it is the same for all. He does not love someone more than others. However, there is a love that is completed and love that is uncompleted. *Everlasting love* is a completed love, a love that is returned and when it is returned it takes on a life of its own, it begins to repeat over and over and become stronger and stronger like the tension of a bow string as the arch pulls back on it. We must recognize that in this case the bow string is God and we are the archer.

God's love is there like a bow string. It has the potential of great power, but until someone pulls back on that bow string, that power is not going to be activated. You can love someone but if they do not love you in return, there will be no love in the relationship. However, when that love is returned then a relationship is established, the power of that love becomes activated and its potential is released.

The difference between a believer and one who is not is not that God loves the believer more, it is simply that the believer returns that love that God has for them and hence activates that love and experiences all the potential that that love has to offer.

God is standing right there, arms wide open loving us. But He cannot love us with an everlasting love (*al ken*) until we return that love to Him. It is now our choice, not God's, He has all the love needed, and has done all the work, and it is now up to us whether we will receive that everlasting love or not.

In my years of searching for God's heart and finding rest in His heart I have learned one thing that millions upon millions have also learned. You can find God's heart, you can find rest in His heart by simply accepting his love and loving Him in return.

OTHER BOOKS
BY CHAIM BENTORAH

HEBREW WORD STUDY—A HEBREW
TEACHER'S SEARCH FOR THE HEART OF GOD

HEBREW WORD STUDY—A HEBREW
TEACHER EXPLORES THE HEART OF GOD

HEBREW WORD STUDY—A HEBREW
TEACHER'S CALL TO SILENCE

BIBLICAL TRUTHS FROM UNCLE OTTO'S FARM

THESE BOOKS ARE AVAILABLE
THROUGH AMAZON.COM
OR
www.chaimbentorah.com

Chaim Bentorah and Chaim Bentorah Ministries are
available for weekend Hebrew classes, conferences
and speaking engagement. Please visit us at www.
chaimbentorah.com for contact information.